THE GOLD GUIDES

TUSCANY

CITIES • TOWNS
MUSEUMS • MASTERPIECES • ART
PARKS • EVENTS

D1407422

BONECHI

Project and design: Casa Editrice Bonechi - *Editorial management*: Monica Bonechi
Project: Monica Bonechi - *Graphic design, picture research, layout and cover by*: Manuela Ranfagni.
Texts by the Casa Editrice Bonechi Editorial Department; pages 120-125, texts by Maria Novella Batini. *Editor*: Mattia Mela
Translations and revised texts by Eve Leckey. *Drawings*: Stefano Benini *(pages 14-15, 19, 22, 24);*
Paolo Fiumi *(pages 46 below, 68-69 below);* Sauro Giampaia *(pages 52 -53, 56-57, 118 below)*

Printed in Italy by *Centro Stampa Editoriale Bonechi.*

The photographs belong to the archive of Casa Editrice Bonechi *and were taken by:* Archivio Fotografico
Toscana Qui (AA.VV./Doriano Ciapetti/Luca del Pia/Italfotogieffe); Gaetano Barone, Carlo Cantini, Serena
De Leonardis, Andrea Fantauzzo, Alessandro Ferrini, Foto Scala, Sergio Galeotti, Roberto Germogli, Paolo
Giambone, Dario Grimoldi, Gianluca Guetta, Silvano Guerrini, Paolo Giambone, Italfotogieffe, Cesare Moroni,
MSA, Nicolò Orsi Battaglini, Andrea Pistolesi, Antonio Quattrone.
Other photographs were provided by: Andrea Innocenti: *pages 110 above, 116 above and center 119 above ;* Atlantide
(Matteo Brogi): *page 38 above;* Atlantide (Guido Cozzi): *pages 38 below, 114 above ;* Atlantide (Massimo Borchi): *pages
124-125 above;* Foto Scala: *pages 40, 53 above, 59 below, 71 below, 76 below, 112 center;* Francesco Giannoni: *pages 49, 50
above and center 83 above, 117 above;* Sergio Galeotti: *pages 54, 57, 59 below ;* Istituzione Giostra del Saracino e Servizio
Giostra del Saracino e folclore, Comune di Arezzo/ Piero Vannuccini *(courtesy of): page 73 center;* Lega del Chianti
(courtesy of): page 46 above ; Fabio Turbanti *(courtesy of): pages 58 center and below, 59 center, 117 center.*

*The publisher apologies for any omissions and is willing to make amends with the formal recognition of
the author of any photo subsequently identified.*

ISBN 978-88-476-1405-5

www. bonechi. com
A   10   9   8   7   6   5   4   3   2   1

GEOGRAPHICAL DESCRIPTION

Located in central Italy, Tuscany covers a surface area of almost 23,000 sq. kilometres and is bordered by Liguria, Emilia Romagna, the Marche and Lazio. Geographically the region is extremely varied with a sandy coast that runs from the north down to Livorno, then becoming rocky as far as the border with Lazio. The hilly interior has some unusual features, such as the Sienese 'crete' (clay hills) and rises to the mountainous area of the Apennines which represent the north east limit of the region, and the Apuan Alps which reach 1,946 metres and dominate the coast around Massa Carrara.

HISTORICAL INTRODUCTION

Etruscan Era

Very little documentary information has come down to us regarding the history of the Etruscans. We know that they had their own language, a religion and customs and traditions, and that politically they were organised into a confederation of twelve cities which were, however, independent from each other. The Etruscan civilization reached its height between the 7th and 5th centuries BC. During this period they founded new centres that developed mainly as a result of

their principle activity in trade and commerce on land and sea. The Etruscans were also skilful at fully exploiting the agricultural fertility of the land as well as its mineral wealth. However, it was precisely due to their economic weakness that they began to decline, when Greek competition for control of the seas became too strong for them. The situation was worsened by the heavy

The "Chimera" of Arezzo (5th cent. B.C.)

defeat suffered at Cuma in 474 BC, internal rebellions such as that of Lazio in 510 BC, and the Gallic invasions.

The Roman and Lombard Era

In the 4th-3rd centuries BC, the Romans asserted their rule over much of the Italic lands, assimilating the customs, organization and culture of the peoples who lived there, as indeed also occurred in the region of Etruria, the future Tuscany. With the fall of the Roman Empire, the region was invaded by the Barbarians and this was followed by a quick succession of various other

9th century BC First traces of an Etruscan presence in Tuscany	474 BC Defeat by the Greeks at Cuma, beginning of the Etruscan decline	205 BC Etruria completely dominated by the Romans.	20 BC Romans found the military colony of Siena
	6th century BC Confederation of the 12 major Etruscan cities	4th century BC (395 BC) Fall of Veio and beginning of the Roman conquest of Etruscan territories	59 BC Romans found Florentia

ETRUSCAN ERA   **ROMAN ERA**

7th-5th century BC
Greatest expansion of the
Etruscan civilization

In 4th-3rd century
BC the Romans
affirm their rule

3

Dante Alighieri (1265-1321)

dioceses such as Arezzo, Pisa, Florence, Pistoia and Siena, gradually increased.

The Communal Era

The Franks dominated following the collapse of Lombard rule and at the end of the 9th century the counts of Lucca were given the title of Marquis of Tuscia. For reasons of succession, at the end of the 11th century Tuscany subsequently became part of the domain of the lords of Canossa. From the 1014 onwards Pisa strengthened its role as a naval and military power in opposition to the Saracens for supremacy of the Ligurian and Tyrrhenian seas. The first consuls were appointed in Pisa in 1080. The decline of the Republic of Pisa was determined in the course of the 13th century

populations until the Lombards confirmed their supremacy in the 6th century. The region was organised into a duchy and Lucca became its centre while the importance and autonomous power of several cities, mainly

both by their defeat at the hands of Genoa at Meloria in 1284, and by the oppressive peace terms imposed when they were conquered by Florence at Fucecchio (1293). From the first half of the 12th century, Siena too appointed consuls, and a republic that supported the Ghibellines came into being, challenging the supremacy of Florence, until they were finally vanquished much later, at the time of the Medici. The death of Mathilde of Canossa in 1115 left a power vacuum and independent groups of citizens began to acquire power, organizing themselves into communes that were controlled by Consuls. With economic growth some cities began to dominate more than others and at the end of the 14th century Florence succeeded in becoming the foremost power. During the 15th century the Medici came to power, controlling the city's government until it

410 Under Alaric the Goths sack and destroy many Tuscan cities	553-569 Byzantine dominion over Tuscany	570 Beginning of Lombard dominion	774-888 Under Charlemagne the Franks create the March of Tuscany	1014 Pisa becomes a naval power
GOTHS	**BYZANTINES**	**LOMBARDS**	**GAULS**	**COMMUNAL ERA**

11th-12th centuries
The Romanesque style develops. The round arch is used in architecture. Sculpture becomes accepted as an independent artistic form

became a grand duchy in the following century.

Medici Rule

Cosimo, the first Medici grand duke, was appointed by the Pope in 1569 and his prime political intention was to conquer and unify Tuscany. In 1555 he finally succeeded in subduing Siena. On becoming grand duke he fortified all the cities under his rule and moreover, on realizing the commercial importance of the port of Livorno, he had it enlarged. Cosimo drained and reclaimed the countryside and introduced new forms of agriculture. Lucca, however, continued to exist quite autonomously and never became part of the grand duchy of Tuscany. In 1574 Francesco I succeeded; more interested in study and research and his private alchemical experiments, he left the task of governing to his ministers. On the other hand, his brother Ferdinando who inherited the throne in 1587 concerned himself with the economic development of Tuscany's cities and the well-being of his citizens. From the 17th century the strength of the grand duchy began to decline and under Cosimo II, Ferdinando II and Cosimo III, its political role was substantially neglected.

The Lorraine and the 19th century

In 1723 Gian Gastone, the last of the Medici dynasty, came to the throne. The succession then passed to the Lorraine family and in the second half of the 18th century under Pietro Leopoldo, Florence enjoyed a new period of glory and of civil and economic progress thanks to the enlightened ideas of the sovereign. In 1808 Tuscany came under Napoleonic rule and the Emperor's sister, Elisa Baciocchi was made grand duchess, but following the Congress of Vienna power was returned to the son of Pietro Leopoldo. In 1860, after some little involvement in the Risorgimento, Tuscany voted for annexation to the kingdom of Italy and Florence became the national capital for a brief interim (1865-1871).

The 20th century

At the beginning of the 20th century the region experienced considerable urban and population growth. These were the years tormented by the "social question", the vindications of the rights of workers and the birth of fascism. In World War II, Tuscany took an active part in the struggle for liberation and, with the end of the war, began an energetic campaign of reconstruction, facilitating speedy industrialization.

Cosimo de' Medici, the Elder (1389-1464)

| 12th century Siena proclaims itself a republic | 1215 The conflict between Guelfs and Ghibellines begins | 1260 Siena defeats the Florentine Guelfs at the battle of Montaperti | 1284 Genoa defeats the Pisans at Meloria — Pisan power begins to decline |

COMMUNAL ERA

1174
Work begins in Pisa on the bell tower

1218
The Abbey of San Galgano, an example of Cistercian Gothic, is founded

HISTORY OF ART

Etruscan and Roman periods

Architecture. *Although there is no trace left of the temples and other religious buildings made of wood by the Etruscans, some Tuscan cities still retain Etruscan stone walls and gateways as can be seen at Roselle, Popolonia, Cortona, Fiesole and Volterra. The best-preserved evidence of the Etruscans and their customs are, however, the necropoli where numerous tombs have survived in good condition. The Romans added theatres to existing structures, such as those in Arezzo, Fiesole and Volterra, and thermal baths, as at Pisa, Volterra and Fiesole.*

Sculpture. *Numerous items of Etruscan sculpture are to be found in museums throughout Tuscany. They were used for funerary purposes, such as the stele with fantastic animals and urns with a figure of the deceased reposing on the cover. The Etruscans also produced works in bronze, such as, the Orator or the Chimera found in Arezzo (Florence Archaeological Museum) as well as the renowned 'bucchero' – black ceramics, typical of ancient Etruria, in forms reproducing the shape of metal plates and dishes. The Romans greatly appreciated these items and at first copied and then adopted them, together with similar Greek items.*

Painting. *A great wealth of Etruscan tomb painting still exists and the subjects most frequently represented are banquets, hunting scenes, games, dancing – all in bright colours making use of strong contrast.*

The Romanesque

Architecture. *The Romanesque style spread throughout Europe in the 11th century; roofs began to be built with barrel and cross vaults replacing wooden beams. In churches the main innovations affected the transept and the ambulatory around the choir. The new style arrived from Lombardy and Emilia and from there spread to other regions. Typical features of the Florentine Romanesque are the external decoration in coloured marble with geometric patterns, as is seen on the Baptistery and San Miniato al Monte. The influence of such examples spread to the area surrounding the city. Pisa, on the other hand, accentuated some of the Lombard architectural elements, such as the small arches, sills and brackets and pilasters. The cathedral, baptistery and bell tower are all examples of this difference. In addition to these characteristics, in Pisa*

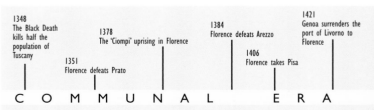

					1421
1348 The Black Death kills half the population of Tuscany		1378 The 'Ciompi' uprising in Florence		1384 Florence defeats Arezzo	Genoa surrenders the port of Livorno to Florence
	1351 Florence defeats Prato			1406 Florence takes Pisa	

C O M M U N A L   E R A

c.1303
Giotto paints the
Ognissanti Madonna

12th century-mid 15th century
Spread of the Gothic style introduced by the Cistercian
monks. Architecture is characterized by an upward thrust
made possible by the use of pointed arches

some oriental influence is present, for example in the bands of black and white marble and mosaic decorative work seen on the façades of the buildings. The Pisan style became quite widely diffused in Lucca and Pistoia. Siena remained somewhat isolated and few traces of Romanesque art remain in the city today, although the surrounding towns and villages provide many examples of this style.

Sculpture. Previously mainly used for the decoration of doorways and capitals, during this period sculpture increasingly came into its own as an art. The human figure was again represented after a long absence, developing the sculptural form within a context that appeared as natural as possible. Pisa was the foremost city to develop this style; Master Guglielmo worked there at this time making the cathedral pulpit, later transferred to the cathedral of

Cagliari, as well as Bonanno Pisano who designed the panels of the San Ranieri Gate (cathedral).

Painting . Of all the art forms, painting was the slowest to develop stylistically, remaining rooted in the Byzantine tradition. Frescoes of this period have disappeared in Tuscany, though some panel paintings and, in particular, wooden crosses still exist.

The Gothic period

Architecture. A new architectural style evolved in northern and central France between 1100 and 1200 and remained widespread throughout Europe until the 14th century. Gothic architecture was characterised by tall, pointed arches that distributed all the weight onto the pillars. Thus the wall between the pillars no longer served as a support and was often replaced by large stained glass windows. Architectural forms came to be based

on the principle of pure simplicity. The romantic ruins of the Cistercian abbey of San Galgano *near Siena* provide an example of this that has survived until today. The architecture of Santa Maria Novella and Santa Croce *in Florence, the* cathedral of Siena *and* Santa Maria della Spina *and the* Camposanto *in Pisa developed from these early buildings. However, their structure lacks the lightness and delicacy of French Gothic since Cistercian architecture preserved the solidity, simplicity and strength*

"François Vase"

of Romanesque structures.

Sculpture. During the 13th century one of the greatest artists in Tuscany was Nicola Pisano who, working in Pisa, entirely renewed the creative spirit that until then had inspired sculptural works. For the baptistery of Pisa and the cathedral of Siena he sculpted bas-reliefs with profoundly human figures in anatomically defined spaces, portrayed with immense power and marked traits.

Painting. During this period Tuscan painting developed in two quite different directions: the Sienese style of Duccio and Simone Martini, and that of Florence, represented by Cimabue and Giotto. As already noted, the artistic circles of Siena were influenced by French art favouring linear and harmonious compositions with delicate colouring. Examples of this are the Maestà by Duccio

Donatello's Habakkuk

now in the Museo dell'Opera del Duomo in Siena, and Simone Martini's fresco of the same subject in the Palazzo Pubblico. From the 1370s Florentine painting had developed in quite a different way. Cimabue's Maestà in the Uffizi still represents a new intensity of expression and sense of space and volume. With Giotto, during the 14th century this new approach spread throughout the peninsula.

The 15th century and Renaissance

Architecture. In the 15th century Florence became the dynamic centre of Tuscany and a new form of art developed here based on complete reassessment of man and of the role played by the fundamental example of classical art. The geometrical rules governing classical masterpieces were revived to reproduce their beauty and harmony. Using these models, the first and greatest Florentine

architect, Brunelleschi, created elegant but majestic architectural structures such as Santo Spirito, San Lorenzo, the Pazzi Chapel, the dome of Santa Maria del Fiore. For about a century all Tuscan architects followed his example: Michelozzo, whose buildings can be seen in Florence, Pistoia, Montepulciano and Volterra; Giuliano da Maiano who worked in Siena: Giuliano da Sangallo in Florence and Prato; Francesco di Giorgio Martini in Cortona.

Sculpture. Sculpture, like architecture, drew its inspiration from the rules underlying classical harmony, and the work of individual artists began to be studied with more attention. Donatello was the sculptor who was most imitated and many artists were influenced by his work: Desiderio da Settignano, Bernardo and Antonio Rossellino, Benedetto da Maiano, Agostino di Duccio, Mino da Fiesole and

1494	1512	1527	1531
The Medici are exiled from Florence, which becomes a republic	Return of the Medici to Florence with Giuliano who reinstates the Signoria	Medici again in exile and the republic is restored	Alessandro de' Medici becomes the first duke of Florence
		1530 Florence is besieged by papal and imperial troops	1555 Siena finally falls under Florentine dominion

MEDICI GRAND DUCHY

1498	1504	1521 Rosso Fiorentino	1550
Savonarola is hanged and burned in Piazza della Signoria	Michelangelo's David is placed in front of the Signoria	paints the deposition in Volterra	Giorgio Vasari publishes the first edition of the "Lives of the Artists"

Luca della Robbia, whose particular talent was expressed in glazed terracotta.

Painting . The Renaissance in painting was introduced by Masaccio who developed the innovations inherited from Giotto almost a century earlier, making use of Brunelleschi's creative perspective and of Donatello's robust sculptural style. The Brancacci chapel in Santa Maria del Carmine in Florence was the school where contemporary painters came to learn, such as Paolo Uccello, for example, as well as Andrea del Castagno and Fra Angelico. However, from the mid 15th century, painters continued to make further innovations, seeking the greater freedom of perspective that can be seen in the work of Piero della Francesca, while also attempting to create a more taut illusion of movement, evident in the style of Verrocchio and Botticelli. Moreover, influenced by the works of Flemish painters that arrived in Florence at the end of the century, Ghirlandaio's works developed the interpretation of the effects of light and colour.

The 16th century

Architecture. Developments in the 16th century were closely linked to the Medici family and their patronage. Thus Florence experienced a period of new constructions while older buildings were transformed, such as the Uffizi or Palazzo Pitti which the Medici refurbished as a palace, while as early as the previous century villas had been built in the surrounding countryside. Moreover, Cosimo I created fortifications in several cities such as Livorno, Pisa, Borgo Sansepolcro and Florence itself where the Fortezza da Basso and Forte Belevedere were built.

Sculpture. As a sculptor the most important personality of the century was without doubt Michelangelo who worked in Florence on various occasions.

Siena

Pistoia

Lucca

Pisa

1569
Cosimo I becomes Grand Duke of Tuscany

1577
Work begins to make Livorno the largest Tuscan port

1737
End of the Medici dynasty. Francis Stephen of Lorraine becomes Grand Duke of Tuscany

1765
Pietro Leopoldo becomes Grand Duke and begins a programme of social reform

MEDICI GRAND DUCHY   **LORRAINE GRAND DUCHY**

1632
Galileo publishes his "Dialolgue concerning the two chief systems of the world" in Florence

1737
Anna Maria Luisa de' Medici stipulates that the Florentine collections must remain in Florence

Pisa

Medici Coat of Arms

Cafaggiolo

Montesiepi

Pistoia

Broli

His work inspired, albeit with different results, Ammannati, Cellini and Giambologna.

Painting. At the turn of the century three of the greatest artists were working in Florence at the same time: Michelangelo, Leonardo and Raphael. But the artistic hegemony for which Florence was renowned began to fade at the end of the first decade, to be replaced by Rome where many artists then decided to move. Towards the 1630s, a group of Florentine artists, later to be known as Mannerists, gave a new impulse to painting and succeeded in restoring some of the prestige lost by the city. Pontormo, Rosso Fiorentino and Bronzino all represent the troubled period in which they lived in the violent colours of paintings that are surprisingly contemporary.

17th and 18th centuries

Architecture. During these centuries Tuscany stagnated somewhat, re-elaborating existing styles and traditions and remaining unaffected by innovation and developments in other Italian or European cities. Patronage and commissions still depended on the Medici.

Sculpture. During this period the best-known personality in the field of sculpture was Pietro Tacca, a sculptor who worked for the Medici court.

Painting. During the period of the1600 and 1700s painting was not altogether mediocre. A few Tuscan personalities such as Cigoli, Cristiano Allori, Santi di Tito and Matteo Rosselli succeeded in modernizing painting

in the region, revising and reviving local traditions. Around 1614 the innovative new work of Caravaggio appeared in Florence with the arrival of the painter Artemisia Gentileschi, a follower of the great master. Beginning in the 1640s, the Medici commissioned Pietro da Cortona to decorate some of the rooms in Palazzo Pitti, while Luca Giordano frescoed part of Palazzo Medici. Both these artists introduced to Florence the grand baroque style which did not, however, reach the level of grandeur that it did in Rome with the patronage of the great aristocratic families.

The 19th century

Architecture. In the 1860s Florence became the capital of the kingdom for a period and consequently it underwent some

1807 Tuscany becomes part of the Napoleonic Empire	1814 The Lorraine return to Tuscany	1847 The Duchy of Lucca is annexed to Tuscany		1865-1871 Florence is capital of the kingdom of Italy
			1860 Plebiscite in Tuscany to become part of the kingdom of Savoy	

LORRAINE GRAND DUCHY   I T A L I A N

1814-1815 Napoleon in exile on the island of Elba	1828 Work begins on reclaiming the land of the Maremma	1841-48 The Florence-Pisa-Livorno railway line is built — the first long distance track in Italy	1862 A new movement of painting begun by the circle of Giovanni Fattori becomes known as the "Macchiaioli"

10

ato

Siena

The Palio

Elba

extensive urban development.

Sculpture. During this century the Accademia di Belle Arti, the school of Fine Arts which had already come into being in the 16th century for students of art, played a fundamental role as it dictated the official culture through a close relationship with the political world, imposing formal rules and iconographic models. All the artists of the time attended it but some managed to break away from the narrow conservatism that the school advocated. Giovanni Dupré or Lorenzo Bartolini, who also taught at the Florentine Academy, advised his pupils to combine traditional Tuscan elements with the neoclassical style in fashion at the time.

Painting. The first few decades were dominated by the academic style

of artists such as Ussi, Ciseri and Benvenuti, but between 1855 and 1867 the Macchiaioli came into being – a group of painters who sought a new method of expressing tones of colour and light more immediately, emotions and expressions more directly, using colour with a speckled effect that created shades closer to reality. They also represented subjects that had been ignored until then, such as landscapes, or farming and rural life. The group was formed of artists such as Fattori, Costa, Signorini, Lega, D'Ancona, Abbati, Sernesi, Zandomeneghi.

The 20th century

Architecture. In Florence, Livorno and Viareggio architecture at the beginning of the century was considerably influenced

by the Art Nouveau style, and was used in many villas and private houses. Important works of a later period are the Artemio Franchi Stadium *in Florence, designed by* Nervi *in 1932, and the* railway station of Santa Maria Novella *designed by* Giovanni Michelucci.

Sculpture. There have been no great or renowned contemporary sculptors in Tuscany. Modigliani, a painter and sculptor from Livorno spent most of his life working in Paris.

Painting. During the 20th century painting was the foremost of the arts, represented by many Tuscan artists who worked both in the region itself and in other European centres, no longer under obligation to a single patron. To mention just a few: Viani, born in Viareggio; Rosai, and Conti, both Florentines; Severini, born in Cortona; Soffici who was from Rignano sull'Arno; Maccari from Siena; Modigliani from Livorno.

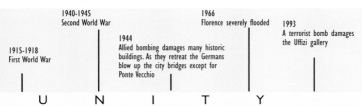

FLORENCE

The city lies in a broad plain crossed by the river Arno and surrounded by hills. In 59 BC the Roman city was founded with the square ground plan of the castrum.

Marcus Aurelius, or perhaps Diocletian, made it the headquarters of the Corrector Italiae, a kind of governor who was responsible for Tuscany and Umbria. With the arrival of the barbarians, Florence was first besieged by the Ostrogoths (405). Next came the Byzantines, who occupied Florence in 539, and the Goths who took over the city in 541. Under Lombard domination (570) it managed to safeguard its autonomy, while under the Franks the number of inhabitants diminished and the city lost most of its territories.

Michelangelo's David

Around the year 1000, the city (whose symbol is a lily) began to expand. In 1183 it became a free commune, even though it had already actually availed itself of this freedom for many years. The first clashes between the two factions, Guelf and Ghibelline, date from this period. The former were followers of the Pope, the latter of the Emperor. The ensuing struggles were to lacerate the civil structure of the city until 1268. Despite the unstable social and political situation, this period witnessed an upsurge in the arts and in literature: this was the time of Dante and his "dolce stil novo", of Giotto and Arnolfo di Cambio. In the 15th century Florence grew as a trading centre but also as the new cradle for Italian, and eventually European,

culture. Many powerful families (the Pitti, Frescobaldi, Strozzi, Albizi) vied for supremacy in the city and one soon took control. The powerful Medici, a family of bankers that began with the founder Cosimo 1, later known as the Elder, were to govern up to the first half of the 18th century, transforming Florence into a beacon during the period of Humanism and the Renaissance. In 1737 the Medicis were succeeded by the house of Lorraine and government continued along the lines of moderate liberalism, though by then the greatest period of Florentine culture was on the wane. In 1860, during the Risorgimento, Tuscany was annexed to the Kingdom of Italy with a plebiscite. Florence then briefly became the capital of the new nation.

DANTE ALIGHIERI

Florence is also the city of Dante Alighieri (1265-1321), father of the Italian language and author of the literary masterpiece the *Divine Comedy*. He is commemorated in the small church of Santa Margherita de' Cerchi and in the Museo Casa di Dante, also near to the church.

The city's historic centre suffered terrible damage during the Second World War and some important buildings were completely destroyed, yet despite this and the flood of 1966 which had such a devastating effect on the urban fabric and structure, the fascination of Florence has survived over the centuries.

The cathedral of Santa Maria del Fiore.

CATHEDRAL OF SANTA MARIA DEL FIORE

On 8 September 1296 Cardinal Pietro Valeriano laid the foundation stone of the cathedral, a structure destined to be completed only after many centuries of work. The design was originally entrusted to Arnolfo di Cambio, and the new cathedral was built over the earlier church of Santa Reparata, which was demolished between 1378 and 1421. Building then proceeded quite rapidly; once the vaulting over the three naves was completed, the tribune and the drum of the dome, part of Arnolfo's original plan, were built. However, construction of the dome proved to be extremely problematic and in 1418 a new competition was announced to decide on its structure. After much debate, the plan presented

Interior of the cathedral (below) and Michelangelo's *Pietà* (left).

by Filippo Brunelleschi was chosen and he completed the dome in 1436. On 25 March of the same year, Pope Eugene IV consecrated the cathedral dedicating it to Santa Maria del Fiore.

Work continued throughout the 15th and 16th centuries on the internal fittings and on the external marble facing. The original **façade** had been designed by Arnolfo di Cambio but in 1587 Grand Duke Francesco I de' Medici had this first design demolished by the architect Bernardo Buontalenti. The present-day façade

is the work of architect Emilio De Fabris (1871-1887).

The **interior** has a sombre Gothic arrangement of a Latin cross with three naves flanked by massive polystyle pillars that support grandiose pointed vaults. Many excellent works of art were made to enhance the interior of the cathedral over the centuries. Some of these, including the magnificent *Pietà* by Michelangelo and the *Choir stalls* by Donatello and Luca della Robbia, are now housed in the Museo dell'Opera del Duomo, though many others are still in their original place. The pavement, made of coloured marbles, was completed in various phases between 1526 and 1660 by numerous artists, one of the greatest being Baccio D'Agnolo.

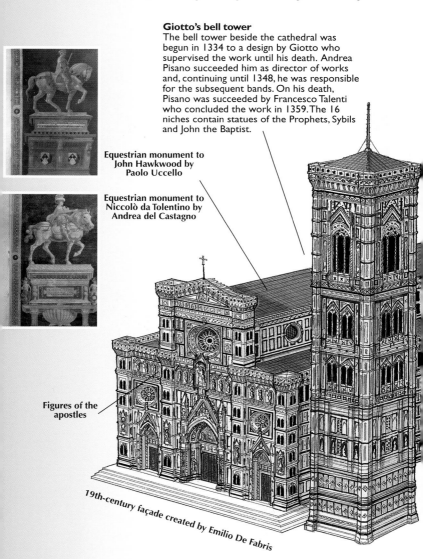

Giotto's bell tower
The bell tower beside the cathedral was begun in 1334 to a design by Giotto who supervised the work until his death. Andrea Pisano succeeded him as director of works and, continuing until 1348, he was responsible for the subsequent bands. On his death, Pisano was succeeded by Francesco Talenti who concluded the work in 1359. The 16 niches contain statues of the Prophets, Sybils and John the Baptist.

Equestrian monument to John Hawkwood by Paolo Uccello

Equestrian monument to Niccolò da Tolentino by Andrea del Castagno

Figures of the apostles

19th-century façade created by Emilio De Fabris

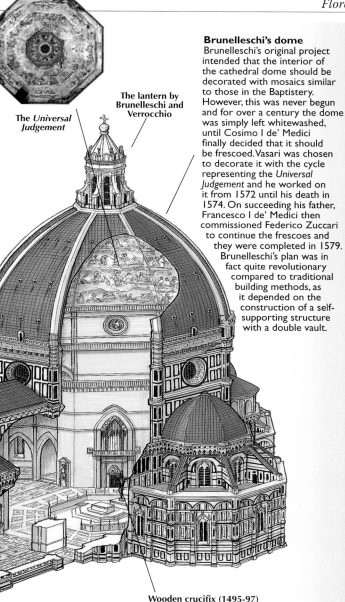

**The lantern by
Brunelleschi and
Verrocchio**

**The *Universal
Judgement***

Brunelleschi's dome
Brunelleschi's original project
intended that the interior of
the cathedral dome should be
decorated with mosaics similar
to those in the Baptistery.
However, this was never begun
and for over a century the dome
was simply left whitewashed,
until Cosimo I de' Medici
finally decided that it should
be frescoed. Vasari was chosen
to decorate it with the cycle
representing the *Universal
Judgement* and he worked on
it from 1572 until his death in
1574. On succeeding his father,
Francesco I de' Medici then
commissioned Federico Zuccari
to continue the frescoes and
they were completed in 1579.
Brunelleschi's plan was in
fact quite revolutionary
compared to traditional
building methods, as
it depended on the
construction of a self-
supporting structure
with a double vault.

Wooden crucifix (1495-97)

Church of Santa Reparata
In 1966 during a programme of excavations,
the remains of the ancient town church
were brought to light: beautiful mosaic
pavements, some frescoes and numerous
tombstones of civil and religious
personalities of medieval and Renaissance
were found, including that of Brunelleschi.

BAPTISTERY – Built over the remains of a building dating from Roman Florence, possibly the Praetorium or a temple dedicated to Mars, the Baptistery was first built as a church dedicated to St John, between the 4th and 5th centuries. The octagonal structure was covered externally with slabs of white and green marble following a precise geometric tripartite pattern. The exterior has three sets of bronze doors: the *North Doors* with *Stories from the New Testament* are by Lorenzo Ghiberti (1403-1424); the *East Doors* known as the *"Gates of Paradise"* are also by Ghiberti; and the third pair, the *South Doors*, are by Andrea Pisano.

The interior is a single large octagonal shaped space richly decorated with polychrome marble and mosaics on a gold ground. A tribune, also known as the **scarsella**, was added to the west side in 1202 and its ceiling was decorated with mosaics representing a wheel by Jacopo, a Franciscan monk. During the 13th century Brother Jacopo also began the mosaics in the dome where Coppo da Marcovaldo was responsible for the *Universal Judgement*.

Below right: the *Story of Adam and Eve*, a panel by Lorenzo Ghiberti for the Gates of Paradise.

Below: the *Baptistery of San Giovanni.*

Lorenzo Ghiberti
Florence 1378 - 1455

The Gates of Paradise

Michelangelo famously called the entrance on the east side of the Baptistery the "Gates of Paradise". The decoration of the two doors has an iconographic cycle that is divided into ten panels of bas-reliefs portraying *Stories of the Old Testament*. These are surrounded by a frame with 24 niches containing statues portraying various *Biblical Characters* and alternating with 24 medallions with *busts of artists*, including a self-portrait of Ghiberti. The original panels are housed in the Museo dell'Opera del Duomo.

PIAZZA DELLA SIGNORIA

The civic administrative centre of Florence, Piazza della Signoria was made on an area where the houses of several powerful Ghibelline families, including the Uberti, and the Foraboschi, stood during the 13th century. After the battle of Benevento (1266) however, these were razed to the ground by the Guelf faction. Along the steps in front of Palazzo Vecchio stand the statues of *Hercules and Cacus*, by Baccio Bandinelli, and Michelangelo's *David*, replaced by a copy in 1873 when the original was removed to the Galleria dell'Accademia. To the far left of the steps is the *Neptune Fountain* by Ammannanti, while in the part of the square where the old commercial tribunal is located stands Giambologna's *Equestrian Monument to Cosimo I*.

Loggia dei Lanzi -Built between 1376 and 1382 by the architects Benci di Cione and Simone Talenti to a design by Orcagna, the loggia was intended to house the most eminent public officials of Florence. However, it is named after the squad of German mercenaries, the Lanzichenecchi, that Grand Duke Cosimo I lodged there as his personal guard.

Subsequently Cosimo I had partitions inserted, transforming the spaces thus obtained into workshops for the artists commissioned to make colossal works of art glorifying the Medici dynasty. Only much later were several classical statues located here, as well as later works such as *Perseus* by Benvenuto Cellini and the *Rape of the Sabines* by Giambologna.

View of Piazza della Signoria (below).
The *Rape of the Sabines* by Giambologna (above)
and *Perseus* by Benvenuto Cellini (right).

PALAZZO VECCHIO

– The most important civic building in medieval Florence, the main nucleus of Palazzo Vecchio was built between 1299 and 1314 as the headquarters of the Priors, the highest office of the Florentine council.

The Salone dei Cinquecento leads to the **Studiolo of Francesco I**, a sophisticated room created by Vasari and richly decorated

The Salone dei Cinquecento (above), the 'Studiolo' of Francesco I (left), *Cherub with a Dolphin* by Verrocchio (below left).

throughout by some of the greatest artists of 16th century Florence. Adjoining are the **Apartments of Leo X**, now the offices of the mayor of Florence, where the stupendous decorations by Vasari include a fresco of the *Siege of Florence*.

On the second floor is the **Sala dei Gigli**, created by Benedetto da Maiano and completed by his brother Giuliano. The room is named after the French fleur-de-lys which decorate the walls, one of which is also enhanced by a fine fresco by Ghirlandaio. The magnificent decorations provide a perfect setting for the bronze group of *Judith and Holofernes*, a masterpiece by Donatello.

The Sala dei Gigli leads to the **Sala dell'Udienza** (Audience Room) through a white marble doorway with a 15th century statue in the lunette of *Justice* by Giuliano and Benedetto da Maiano; also located here are the **Apartments of Eleonora di Toledo**. A small passageway leads to the **Quartieri degli Elementi**, named after the **Sala degli Elementi** (Room of the Elements) which has walls frescoed by Vasari with allegories of the four elements. Other rooms here of especial interest are the **Hercules Room** and the **Juno Loggia** where the original of Verrocchio's *Cherub with a Dolphin* is housed.

Equestrian monument to Cosimo I

ARNOLFO'S TOWER

Arnolfo di Cambio built the tower of
Palazzo Vecchio on the pre-existing
Torre della Vacca, once the property
of the Foraboschi family and in
13th century the only tower house
surviving in this area. The structure
is some 94 metres in height. The bell
tower is crowned by a bronze spire
dating from the mid 15th century,
from which rises a pole bearing
a fleur-de-lys and lion rampant,
emblems of the city of Florence.

The lion rampant
bearing the lily,
symbol of Florence

Arnolfo's
tower

Frescoes of the
nine coats of arms
of the Florentine
Republic

Salone dei
Cinquecento

Uffizi Gallery

Perseus by
Benvenuto
Cellini

Loggia dei Lanzi

Copy of the David

Arnolfo's
courtyard

Neptune Fountain
by Bartolomeo
Ammannati

ARNOLFO'S COURTYARD

The interior of Palazzo Vecchio is approached
through the **courtyard** made by Arnolfo di
Cambio and refurbished in 1470 by Michelozzo
who enhanced it with a portico. In the place of
the old well in the centre, Grand Duke Cosimo
I had an elegant fountain made, decorated with
a *Cherub with a Dolphin*, the original of which is
now located in one of the palace rooms.

19

THE "PORCELLINO"

The "porcellino", or little pig, that stands on one side of the New Market (1547) where once luxury items were sold, is in fact a boar made by Pietro Tacca in 1639. It is widely believed that stroking his nose will bring good luck and tradition maintains that one should make a wish while touching his snout, then placing a coin in the animal's mouth. Should the coin fall straight into the grating below the wish will come true.

PONTE VECCHIO – This is the oldest bridge over the river Arno and probably already existed at the time of Roman *Florentia* for traffic coming from the Via Cassia. The bridge was swept away in the flood of 1177 and again in 1333. It is believed that the present bridge was built to a design by Taddeo Gaddi in 1345. This three-span structure had arches along the parapets beneath which many small shops were located, once mainly occupied by butchers. However, in the 16th century Ferdinando I de' Medici requisitioned these for the goldsmiths who in the course of time enlarged their shops, building the characteristic houses that project over the river. Benvenuto Cellini was chosen to represent the new residents and business of the bridge and is portrayed in a bronze bust (1900) by Raffaele Romanelli on the decorative fountain in the centre.

The elegant arches of Ponte Vecchio.

HISTORY OF THE UFFIZI GALLERY

The Uffizi Palace was commissioned from Giorgio Vasari by Cosimo I de' Medici in 1560 and the original project was completed by Alfonso Parigi and Bernardo Buontalenti in 1580. Built beside the newly enlarged Palazzo Vecchio, it was intended to house the offices of the city's magistracy. The U shaped structure, grandly arrayed along the banks of the Arno, entailed the loss of a beautiful old church, San Piero a Scheraggio, which was partly demolished and partly incorporated into the new building. On the ground floor Vasari created a lofty portico with a loggia above. Cosimo's successor, Francesco I, converted the Palace into a gallery, commissioning Buontalenti to build the Tribune where the Grand Duke could display his collection of antique items and medallions. Francesco also had the first corridor of the gallery arranged to house the Greek and Roman statues belonging to the Medici, giving it the name of Gallery of the Statues. Following the death of Francesco, Ferdinando I de' Medici had the antique classical statues from Villa Medici in Rome transferred to Florence, further enriching the collection. Other important acquisitions were made during the 17th century

under Ferdinando II, whose wife, Vittoria della Rovere, brought as her dowry the substantial patrimony of her grandfather, Federico Duke of Urbino, including works by such artists as Raphael and Titian. However, the most important contribution to the Medici Collections was the bequest of Cardinal Leopoldo to his nephew, Cosimo III de' Medici who had new rooms and cabinets built to house them, at the same time making a grander, more monumental entrance to the Uffizi. His daughter, Anna Maria Luisa, last of the Medici dynasty and widow of the Palatine Elector, added works by German and Flemish artists and, with the Family Pact of 1737, ensured that the Lorraine would leave the art collections that had been created by her family for the permanent enjoyment of the citizens of Florence. The Uffizi Gallery thus became the first civic art museum, destined to grow and develop over the course of time, and resulting in the creation of other prestigious Florentine museums.

UFFIZI GALLERY

Since the 16th century the Gallery has continually evolved and now also incorporates part of the Vasari Corridor. The rooms housing paintings are generally arranged in chronological order, so that the sections correspond to the century in which the works were produced:

- 13th and 14th centuries (Duecento, Trecento)
- 15th century (Quattrocento)
- Northern European Painting
- The Tribune
- 16th century (Cinquecento)
- 17th and 18th centuries (Seicento, Settecento).

Duecento and Trecento
Duccio di Buoninsegna
Madonna Rucellai
(Room 2)

Duecento and Trecento
Giotto
Madonna di Ognissanti
(Room 2)

21

Duecento and Trecento
Simone Martini e
Lippo Memmi
Annunciation (Room 3)

Quattrocento
Leonardo da Vinci
Annunciation
(Room 15)

Quattrocento
Gentile da Fabriano
Adoration of the Magi
(Room 5-6)

Cinquecento
Michelangelo Buonarroti
Tondo Doni (Room 25)

Quattrocento
Paolo Uccello
Battle of San Romano
(Room 7)

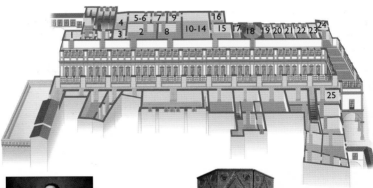

Tribune
Bronzino
*Portrait of Eleonora di
Toledo with her son
Giovanni*
(Room 18)

Quattrocento
Filippo Lippi
*Virgin and Child
with Angels*
(Room 8)

Duecento and
Trecento
L'Orcagna
Jacopo di Cione
*Saint Matthew and
Stories from his Life*
(Room 4)

Quattrocento
Luca Signorelli
The Holy Family
(Room 19)

Botticelli (Sandro Filipepi), Florence 1445-1510

Birth of Venus
Tempera, 172x278.5 1484-86

The subject is probably taken from Ovid's "Metamorphoses" and the "Fasti" – where Time is described as offering a cloak to Venus – and therefore reflects themes from the literature of Humanism in general.

Primavera
Tempera, 203x314 1482-83

This painting is probably the most popular and exploited of Botticelli's works. Vasari saw it when it was located in Cosimo I's Villa at Castello. On the right, Zephyr pursues the nymph Chloris who is transformed into the goddess Flora, scattering flowers across the world. In the centre, Venus represents Charity to whom the Humanists in Medici circles also attributed other characteristics; on the left are the Three Graces dancing and Mercury who chases away the clouds.

Cinquecento
Raphael
*Madonna of the
Goldfinch*
(Room 26)

Cinquecento
Titian
The Urbino Venus
(Room 28)

Cinquecento
Parmigianino
*Virgin and Child with
Saints (Saint Zachary)*
(Room 29)

Cinquecento
Veronese
Annunciation
(Room 31)

Cinquecento
Pontormo
*The Supper at
Emmaus* (Room 27)

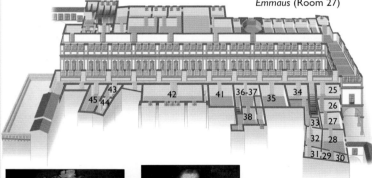

Seicento and Settecento
Caravaggio
Bacchus
(Room 43)

Seicento and Settecento
Rembrandt
Portrait of an Old Man
(Room 44)

Cinquecento
Tintoretto
Leda and the Swan
(Room 32)

VASARI CORRIDOR

Vasari managed to build this raised passageway linking the Uffizi to Palazzo Pitti in just five months for Cosimo I de' Medici. The corridor crosses the Arno running above Ponte Vecchio and, after passing around instead of through the Mannelli Tower, it crosses the Santa Felicità church and then arrives at Palazzo Pitti. Displayed along the Corridor are many 17th and 18th century works, as well as a large collection of artists' self portraits from the 16th to 20th centuries.

PALAZZO PITTI AND ITS MUSEUMS

The palace, begun in 1457 by the architect Luca Fanelli following a design by Brunelleschi, was bought in 1549 by Eleonora di Toledo, wife of Cosimo I de' Medici, who commissioned Ammannati to undertake the task of enlargement (1558-1577). During the first half of the 17th century, Giulio and Alfonso Parigi further extended the palace; in the 18th century the two wings with porticos and terraces, known as the Rondò, were added and lastly in the neo-classical period the **Palazzina della Meridiana** was built and now houses the **Costume Gallery** and the **Contini Bonacossi Donation** of paintings, sculptures and Della Robbia works dating from the 15th to the 16th centuries.

The palace passed to the Savoy family who lived here during the period when Florence was capital of the new kingdom. In 1919 king Vittorio Emanuele III donated the palace and all its contents to the Italian state which initiated the organization of the collections and possessions bringing four different museums into existence: the **Palatine Gallery**, the **Gallery of Modern Art**, the **Silver Museum**, and the **Carriage Museum**. The **Royal Apartments** were later restored and opened to the public. The works belonging to the Palatine Gallery are exhibited in sumptuous salons and are arranged according to criteria adopted for the creation of a gallery intended for the personal and family use of the Medici and Lorraine Houses. Cosimo II de' Medici and his son Ferdinando II created this splendid picture gallery during the second half

The façade of Pitti Palace.

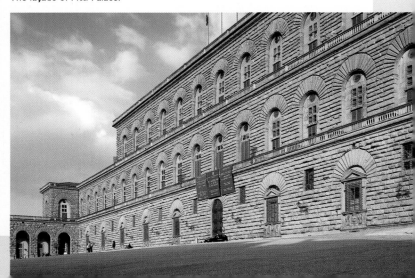

Madonna and Child by Filippo Lippi.

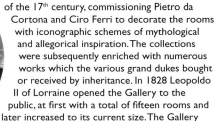

of the 17th century, commissioning Pietro da Cortona and Ciro Ferri to decorate the rooms with iconographic schemes of mythological and allegorical inspiration. The collections were subsequently enriched with numerous works which the various grand dukes bought or received by inheritance. In 1828 Leopoldo II of Lorraine opened the Gallery to the public, at first with a total of fifteen rooms and later increased to its current size. The Gallery contains many works entirely representing the artistic scene between the 15th and 18th centuries; one of the most important groups of works is that consisting of Titian's paintings, such as the *Concert*, and Raphael's works, including some famous portraits such as the *Fornarina, Maddalena Doni* and *La Gravida* as well as some religious subjects – the *Madonna of the Grand Duke*, the *Madonna della Seggiola* (the chair), the *Madonna dell'Impannata* (the window) and the *Vision of Ezekiel*. The Florentine school is represented by Filippo Lippi (*Madonna and Child*) and Andrea del Sarto (*Assumption of the Virgin with Apostles and Saints*, the *Holy Family* and *Stories of Joseph*). The Italian 17th century is also well represented with important works such as the *Sleeping Cupid* by Caravaggio, while northern European art is also present with, for example, Rubens paintings of the *Four Philosophers* and the *Consequences of War*.

The **Gallery of Modern Art** is on the second floor

Madonna della Seggiola by Raphael.

Madonna of the Grand Duke by Raphael.

'*La Fornarina*' by Raphael.

of Palazzo Pitti and contains over two thousand sculptures and paintings by artists working from the early 19th century to the first decades of the 20th century. In **Room VI** is the fine *Bust of Napoleon* made by Canova; **Room X** houses a large sculptural group portraying *Cain and Abel* by Dupré; in **Room XV** are works by Giovanni Boldini; exhibited in **Rooms XXIII** and **XXIV** is a fine collection of "Macchiaioli"painting with works by all the most important artists of that movement: Giovanni Fattori, Silvestro Lega, Giuseppe Abbati, Telemaco Signorini, Cristiano Banti, Edoardo Borrani, Vincenzo Cabianca, Cesare Ciani to mention only a few.

The Concert by Titian.

The **Museo degli Argenti** (Silver Museum) contains secular and religious gold and silver work, ivory, vases made of semi-precious stone and rock crystal. Also displayed is Lorenzo il Magnifico's collection of vases, with the magnificent *lapis lazuli vase* by Bilivert alongside the pieces of *German ivory* from the collection of prince Mattia de' Medici. Also interesting are the rare *jewels* and precious little '*galanterie*' or favours, belonging to Anna Maria Luisa, the last descendant of the Medici. Eleonora di Toledo created the magnificent **Boboli Gardens**. Tribolo began work on them in 1550, followed by Ammannati and then Buontalenti who worked on them from 1583 on. He created the **Grotta del Buontalenti** and in 1585 Michelangelo's *Prisoners* were placed here; now replaced by copies, the originals are in the Accademia Gallery. Lying beyond the courtyard of Palazzo Pitti is the theatrical **Amphitheatre**, made by Alfonzo Parigi in the 17th century, where a large *grey granite basin* from the Baths of Caracalla in Rome and an *Egyptian obelisk* from the Temple of Amun in Thebes are to be found. The **Porcelain Museum** is located in the **Palazzina del Cavaliere**.

Sleeping Cupid by Caravaggio.

The Four Philosophers by Rubens.

Masaccio's *Trinity* (left); the Green Cloister (above); the church of Santa Maria Novella showing the façade designed by Alberti.

CHURCH AND MONASTERY OF SANTA MARIA NOVELLA - The grand and lofty **interior** is in the typical Cistercian style that was adopted for Florentine religious buildings during the 13th century. With the passing of time the wealthiest Florentine families financed the enlargement of the church and monastery, building in addition numerous chapels where members of these illustrious houses were buried. Amongst these chapels are the **Chapel of Filippo Strozzi**, frescoed by Filippino Lippi; the **Great Chapel**, decorated with frescoes by Domenico Ghirlandaio and the **Gondi Chapel**, housing *Brunelleschi's Crucifix*, the only wooden sculpture by this famous artist. In the left nave is one of the greatest works of art not only in Santa Maria Novella, but of all 15th-century Florentine painting: Masaccio's *Trinità*, dated 1427. A most beautiful recently restored *Crucifix* now hangs above the central nave. The lower part of the **façade** was begun in the 14th century and was completed in 1470 by Leon Battista Alberti.

The **monastery** surrounds two large cloisters. The **Chiostro Verde** (Green Cloister) was built in the mid 14th century and was still influenced by the Romanesque style. The name is derived from the frescoes portraying Stories of the Old Testament executed in the first half of

the 15th century by Paolo Uccello in *terra verde* and now housed in the adjacent Refectory.

The **Chiostro Grande**, completely frescoed with works by the greatest Tuscan artists of the 16th and 17th centuries, is reached from here. Access to the **Spanish Chapel** is from the north side of the Chiostro Verde.

Originally the Chapter House of the Dominican Monastery, it was built in the mid 14th century according to a plan by Jacopo Talenti. In 1540 Eleonora di Toledo, the Spanish wife of Cosimo I de' Medici, had it converted into a chapel so that her Spanish courtiers could use it for their worship.

Allegory of the Church Militant
by Andrea di Bonaiuto in the Spanish Chapel.

FRESCO CYCLE IN THE SPANISH CHAPEL

The interior of the Chapel was entirely decorated by Andrea di Buonaiuto, who painted a complex fresco cycle (1355-1357) mainly inspired by the *"Mirror of True Penitence"*, a treatise written by the Prior of the monastery, Brother Jacopo Passavanti, for the purpose of glorifying the Dominican Order.

On the wall opposite the entrance the sacrifice of Christ is recounted in three scenes: the *road to Calvary, Crucifixion* and *Descent to Limbo*. The vault is divided into four segments representing the triumph of Christ over death (*Resurrection* and *Ascension*) and the Apostles' first missions for the church (the *Apostles' boat* and *Pentecost*).

On the right wall is the great *Allegory of the Church Militant* in which the missions and triumph of the Dominicans are represented. In front of the 14th-century image of how the Cathedral would

eventually appear, stand the civil and religious authorities together with the pope and emperor, governing the people and followers of Christianity, defended by black and white dogs, the emblem of the Dominicans (*Domini Canes*, meaning the dogs of our Lord). In the distance St Dominic, St Thomas of Aquinas and St Peter Martyr contest the heretics while dogs at their feet (also black and white) tear wolves, symbolising the heretics, to pieces. Above, the example of earthly pleasures, represented by a group of ladies and gentlemen dancing, is counterbalanced by that of penitence, the only true way to paradise, indicated by St Dominic. The worthy are welcomed in Paradise by St Peter and by two angels crowning the blessed who will be admitted to the presence of Christ in Glory. Illustrated on the left wall is the *Triumph of Saint Thomas of Aquinas.*

CHURCH OF SAN LORENZO AND THE MEDICI CHAPELS -

This is the oldest church in Florence and was consecrated in 393 by St Ambrose. The existing building was financed principally by the Medici family who in 1419 commissioned Filippo Brunelleschi to supervise construction of the extended building, a task that was continued after his death by his pupil Andrea Manetti, and was completed in 1460. Michelangelo was called on to design and build the façade. In 1518 he initiated an ambitious project that was only partially begun on the inside with the building of a *gallery* where reliquaries were exhibited. Externally the church remained quite without its façade. Inside are two *bronze pulpits* by Donatello who also worked on the decoration of the **Old Sacristy**, designed by Brunelleschi and reached from the left transept. Beside the basilica is an elegant **cloister** on the far side of which is the entrance to the **Laurentian Library**.

MEDICI CHAPELS –

This complex of buildings is the mausoleum of the Medici family. There are two main sections: the **Chapel of the Princes** and the **New Sacristy**. In addition there is a vast **crypt** with the tombstones of various Medici princes. Beneath the church are the *tombs of Cosimo the Elder and Donatello*.

The unfinished façade of the church of San Lorenzo in Florence.

One of Donatello's bronze pulpits.

Interior of the church of San Lorenzo.

Interior of the Chapel of the Princes
and the allegorical statues sculpted by
Michelangelo for the New Sacristy.

Dawn

New Sacristy – Michelangelo created this space about 1520, completely in contrast to the harmonious balance of Brunelleschi's Old Sacristy inside San Lorenzo and charged with a feeling of dynamism and energy that resonates in the decoration of the walls. The *tomb of Lorenzo, Duke of Urbino* and nephew of Lorenzo il Magnifico, has a *statue of the Duke* in the central niche above the sarcophagus. Two more statues, *Dawn* and *Dusk,* are symmetrically arranged on the volutes of the funerary urn below. The *tomb of Giuliano,* Duke of Nemours and third son of Lorenzo il Magnifico has statues of *Day* and *Night* on the urn which, together with the images of Dawn and Dusk, represent an overall allegory of the transience of time and the inconsistency of man's life. The *statue of Duke Giuliano* is an idealised image of a youthful and courageous warrior. The mortal remains of Lorenzo il Magnifico and his brother, Giuliano, were arranged by Vasari in a simple tomb with a sculptural group by Michelangelo on top portraying the *Madonna and Child*, flanked by images of *Saints Cosma and Damiano*.

Day

Dusk

Chapel of the Princes – Begun by Matteo Nigetti in the early 1600s century and only completed in the following century, the style of this sumptuous architectural work perhaps represents the finest example in Florence of the creative fantasy of baroque design. The dome, similar to that in the cathedral, was entirely frescoed in the first half of the 19th century with *Biblical Scenes*. Dominating the chapel are six great Medici *tombs*, built for the burial of the Medici grand dukes: Cosimo I, Francesco I, Ferdinando I and Cosimo II de' Medici who are, however, buried in the crypt.

Night

ACCADEMIA GALLERY

The Lorraine Grand Duke Pietro Leopoldo created the Accademia in 1784 furnishing it with not only some most beautiful statues but also an important collection of paintings which was further increased by the works of art removed from religious institutions. Much of the immense popularity of the Accademia Gallery is due to the statues by Michelangelo housed here – the *Prisoners* (or *Slaves*), *St Matthew* and especially the *David* which underwent restoration in 2004. The highly sophisticated procedure made use of the latest techniques in order to preserve intact the patina of the work's 500 year existence and the result has been praised for the delicacy of the operation which preserved a David that is still entirely familiar to his public.

The Gallery houses works of Florentine art dating from the 13th to the 16th centuries: a *Madonna and Child* by Lorenzo Monaco, a renowned early Renaissance Florentine cassone **panel** painted with *scenes of a wedding party*, and the *Madonna del Mare* (of the Sea) attributed to Botticelli. The newly arranged **Medici and Lorraine collection of musical instruments** belonging to the Cherubini Conservatory of Music is worth a visit.

Atlantis

The *"Pietà di Palestrina"*

Young prisoner

Bearded prisoner

Michelangelo
Caprese 1475 - Rome 1564

The David
Marble, 1502-1504

It took months of hard work between 1502 and 1504 for Michelangelo to create his masterpiece in polished marble. David symbolises physical and moral integrity and strength and was originally located in front of Palazzo Vecchio to represent the will to defend the civil and political independence of the Florentine Republic. The biblical character is caught at the instant of greatest tension, anticipating the encounter with his enemy and before he can claim victory over Goliath with his foot planted firmly on the head of the vanquished.

BARGELLO NATIONAL SCULPTURE MUSEUM

Designed by two Dominican monks, Sisto and Ristoro, the Bargello palace was built in 1255 as the headquarters of the Capitano del Popolo. In 1261 it became the magistrates' palace and from 1502 it housed the Council, or Tribunal, of Justice until becoming the residence in 1574 of the Chief Magistrate, also known as the Bargello from the Latin *bargildus*, an office that existed during the Carolingian period. The building now houses the **National Museum of the Bargello**.

Bronze figure of
Perseus

The walls of the **courtyard** are quite literally covered with *coats of arms* of the magistrates, districts and sectors of the city, mainly 19ᵗʰ century reproductions. Along the west wall is the **monumental stairway**, designed by Neri di Fioravanti (1345-1367) with, at the lower end, a stone *Marzocco*, the lion symbol of Florence. Above is the **balcony**, a real architectural gem attributed to Tone di Giovanni (1319). By the stairway on the ground floor is the **Michelangelo and 16ᵗʰ century sculpture Room**, housing *Bacchus*, *Brutus*, *Apollo* (or David) and the *Pitti Tondo* all by Michelangelo as well as Sansovino's *Bacchus*, a *Bust of Cosimo I* by Baccio Bandinelli, another *Bust of Cosimo I* by Cellini, numerous *bronzes* made by Cellini for the *Perseus* sculptural group, and *Hermes* by Giambologna. The **Medieval Sculpture Room** is on the other side of the courtyard and contains sculptures, bas-reliefs and architectural elements from religious buildings and monuments in the area around Florence.

The *Pitti Tondo*

On the first floor the **Donatello Room**, or **Audience Room**, contains more interesting pieces, including two lovely terracottas by Luca della Robbia, as well as Donatello's famous *David*, and two panels with the *Sacrifice of Isaac*, one by Ghiberti and one by Brunelleschi, made for the competition for the Baptistery Doors held in 1401.
The minor arts are displayed in several other rooms, such as the **Carrand Room** and the **Maiolica Room**. One of the most interesting rooms on the second floor is dedicated to **Giovanni della Robbia**, and as well as various terracottas, his charming *Pietà* is exhibited here.

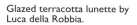

Glazed terracotta lunette by Luca della Robbia.

33

View and interior of the church of Santa Croce in Florence.

CHURCH AND MONASTERY OF SANTA CROCE - The original church of Santa Croce was built by the Minorite order of St Francis about 1228, and work on the new and larger basilica began in 1294. Arnolfo di Cambio worked on the church, a monumental Gothic structure entirely in harmony with Franciscan ideals. Michelozzo carried out the last project to further enlarge the building during the first half of the 15th century.

The façade was completed in the mid 19th century to a design by Nicolò Matas. Gaetano Baccani was responsible for the bell tower which also dates from the 19th century.

The church – The church has been the burial place for members of the most important Florentine nobility and famous personalities since the 14th century. As well as the *Dante Cenotaph* and the *tombs of Ugo Foscolo* and *Vittorio Alfieri*, a *Monument to Michelangelo* and a *Funerary Monument to Galileo* are located here.

At the right end of the transept, beside the door that leads into the sacristy, is the **Baroncelli Chapel**, frescoed by Taddeo Gaddi with *Scenes from the Life of Mary* and decorated with a *Coronation of the Virgin*, a polyptych attributed to Giotto's workshop. The frescoes of *Scenes from the Life of St Francis of Assisi* in the **Bardi Chapel** (1318) and the *Scenes from the Life of St John the Baptist* in the **Peruzzi Chapel** (1320) are by Giotto. Vasari made alterations to the original Gothic structure in 1560 destroying some fine and rare works of art. The wonderful 15th-century aedicule in the right nave, sculpted by Donatello and portraying the *Annunciation*, was saved however. The **Main Chapel** with stained glass designed by Agnolo Gaddi was entirely

Polyptych on the high altar of the church of Santa Croce.

frescoed around 1380 also by Gaddi who illustrated the walls with the *Legend of the True Cross*. The frescoes on the right side of the **Sacristy** are quite lovely, representing a splendid *Crucifixion* by Taddeo Gaddi in the centre, with the *Road to Calvary* attributed to Spinello Aretino on one side and the *Resurrection* by Niccolò Gerini on the other. Access to the 14th-century **Rinucci Chapel** is from the Sacristy; frescoed by Giovanni da Milano with *Scenes from the Life of Mary Magdalene* and *Scenes from the Life of the Virgin* (1363-1366), the Chapel also houses a lovely polyptych representing the *Virgin with Child and Saints*.

The Monastery – The buildings extend around two cloisters to the right side of the church. In the first of these is one of the greatest masterpieces of Florentine Renaissance architecture – the **Pazzi Chapel** by Brunelleschi.

The former Franciscan monastery, including the old **Refectory**, now houses the **Museo dell'Opera di Santa Croce** where some of the most important 13th-century Florentine works of art are exhibited, the most impressive being the monumental *Crucifix* by Cimabue. The wall at the far end is completely frescoed with six scenes painted by Taddeo Gaddi, including the *Last Supper* which extends below the immense *Tree of the Cross*.

Pazzi Chapel – This is one of Filippo Brunelleschi's most original works. Commissioned by Andrea Pazzi, a member of one of the most illustrious Florentine families, Brunelleschi began work on the building in 1443. He managed to complete the pronaos, but not the entire façade, before his death as well as imposing his particular style on the interior. The decorative elements here consist of Della Robbia's polychrome tondos which enhance the pendentives in the dome and the walls. The first four represent the *Evangelists* and

were probably designed by Brunelleschi himself, while the white and blue ceramic roundels portraying the *Apostles* are the work of Luca della Robbia.

The *Baroncelli Chapel* showing the frescoes by Taddeo Gaddi, Church of Santa Croce.

Cimabue
(Cenni di Pepo)
Florence c. 1240 - Pisa 1302

Crucifix
Tempera

Cimabue's Crucifix, exhibited in the Refectory of Santa Croce was severely damaged in the flood that occurred in Florence in 1966 and for long was an icon of the city afflicted by this terrible event.

VIALE DEI COLLI AND PIAZZALE MICHELANGELO

The Viale dei Colli winds for about six kilometres around the hills on the south side of the city. It was designed in 1868 by Giuseppe Poggi, the architect who also made the plans for **Piazzale Michelangelo**, an enormous terrace overlooking Florence. In the piazzale are copies of Michelangelo's sculptures: *David* and the four *allegorical figures* on the Medici tombs in the New Sacristy of San Lorenzo. On one side, a little higher than the piazzale, is the Coffee House (Palazzina del Caffé, 1873), also by Poggi, partially obscuring the approach to the churches of San Salvatore and San Miniato al Monte.

ous buildings connected to them, as well as a large structure with crenulations, the **Palazzo degli Studi**, intended to serve as a college where young Florentine men could study the liberal arts. The **main church** is a large building with a single nave and cross vaulted ceiling, while the second church, the **Certosa**, has a Greek cross plan. The other buildings of the Certosa, and in particular the **Cloisters**, are generally in Renaissance style.

Above, a panorama of Florence from Piazzale Michelangelo. Below: aerial view of the Certosa at Galluzzo.

CERTOSA OF GALLUZZO

The Certosa at Galluzzo, also known as the Certosa of Florence in the Ema Valley, was founded by Niccolò Acciaiuoli in the late 14th century and stands at the top of a hill near where the river Ema meets the Greve. It consists of two churches and vari-

FIESOLE

This ancient city of Etruscan origin stands at the top of a hill overlooking Florence. The town centres around the lovely **Piazza Mino da Fiesole** where the **Cathedral of S. Romolo**, dating from the 11th century, stands. Inside is the fine Cappella Salutati, frescoed in the 15th century by Cosimo Rosselli and the *Tomb of Bishop Salutati* by Mino da Fiesole. The **Palazzo Vescovile** and the old **Church of Santa Maria Primerana** also face onto the square. A street here climbs up to the church of Sant'Alessandro and the **Church** and **Franciscan Convent**, which houses the **Ethnographic Mission Museum** containing important Etruscan artefacts. It is a short walk from the piazza to the **Archaeological site** and **Museo Civico Archeologico**, as well as the lovely **Roman Theatre** dating from the first century BC, where frequent theatre and cinema seasons are held. Nearby are the **Roman Baths** and the **Etrusco-Roman Temple**. Not to be forgotten is the fine **Museo Bandini** which houses sculpture and painting from the 13th to 15th centuries.

VINCI

Vinci is known throughout the world as the place where Leonardo da Vinci was born and every year here on 15 April he is commemorated with celebrations and cultural events. The old **church of the Holy Cross** still houses the baptismal font where he was christened.

The **Da Vinci Museum** is housed in two large rooms on the ground floor of the **Conti Guidi Castle** and exhibits drawings, paintings and models of machines designed by Leonardo.

Also of interest are the **Biblioteca Leonardiana**, an important centre for study and research into the works of this great artist and scientist, and in nearby Anchiano the house where Leonardo was born is open to the public.

Wind surfing on the Bilancino lake.

BARBERINO DI MUGELLO

Not far from Florence, the town and environs of Barberino di Mugello lie in the upper regions of the Sieve valley, which starts near Montecuccioli. Although the area is mainly mountainous and the valley was marshy until the early modern period, ancient peoples lived in this area even before the Etruscans. In the piazza at the centre of the town are **Palazzo Pretorio**, dating from the 15th century and now with a neo-Medieval appearance after restoration in the 19th century, and the **Medici Loggia**, created by Michelozzo between the 14th and 15th centuries, as an annex to the market square. In the countryside near to Barberino is the **Bilancino Lake**, an important source of water for the area and a tourist attraction during the summer months.

Panorama of Barberino di Mugello.

BORGO SAN LORENZO

The town is in the centre of the Mugello, straddling the Sieve, and extends from the Apennine chain to the slopes surrounding the Florentine valley to the north- west. There are numerous places of interest including the **Oratory of the Miraculous Holy Crucifix**, built to house a *wood crucifix*, probably the work of Giovanni Pisano, and the **parish church of San Lorenzo**, dating from 941. This is probably the largest Romanesque building in the environs of Florence and, among other items, it houses works attributed to Giotto and by Matteo Rosselli.

Tabernacle of Saint Francis beside the parish church of San Lorenzo.

SCARPERIA

Originally built as a castle for the strategic protection of the city of Florence, the 14th century **Palazzo dei Vicari** is the symbol of Scarperia. In the 15th century it became the seat of a Vicariato of the Florentine Republic. Over time the palace acquired the numerous coats of arms of the vicars who occupied the palace. These emblems now decorate the façade and atrium, together with many frescoes and antique furnishings. The palace also houses a **Museum of knife-making.**

View of Scarperia.

MUSEUM OF CUTTING TOOLS

One of the most important attractions of Scarperia is the Museo dei Ferri Taglienti (literally "cutting tools") which is related to the traditional industry of knife-making practised in this town for many centuries. Opened with the present layout in 1999 and divided into five sections, the museum provides an educational introduction to the craft of knife-making including the history of "cutting tools" and information regarding the trade and processes, from the centres of production in Italy to the cutlers of Scarperia.

PRATO

The city of Prato is situated on the plain between Pistoia and Florence, on the right bank of the Bisenzio river.

Herod's banquet by Filippo Lippi in the choir of Prato cathedral.

In the 12th century Prato became a free commune. It was at this time that, despite the competition of Florence on one side and Pistoia on the other, the city began to develop both economically and artistically. In 1351 it came under the dominion of Florence. In 1653 Prato gained the statute of city and became a diocese. Today Prato is the largest industrial centre in the hinterland of Florence.

CATHEDRAL OF SANTO STEFANO – Dated 10th century, the **façade** is of coloured marble and was created between 1385 and 1456. On the right corner is the impressive and renowned *Pulpit of the Holy Girdle*, a work by Donatello and Michelozzo. The beautiful *Dancing Putti* around the parapet, now replaced by a copy, is by Donatello. On the main altar is a beautiful bronze crucifix by Ferdinando Tacca (1653). The cycle of fresco in the choir is by Filippo Lippi. At the left end of the transept is the **Chapel of the Holy Girdle** (1385-95) where the *Legend of the Holy Girdle* is represented around the walls in the fresco cycle by Agnolo Gaddi (1392-95). On the altar is a statue of the *Virgin and Child*, a masterpiece by Giovanni Pisano (1317); near the be-

ginning of the right nave is a very fine wooden *crucifix* by Giovanni Pisano.

CASTLE OF THE EMPEROR – More unique than rare in Tuscany, the structure of the Castle of the Emperor, or St Barbara Fortress, is a pure example of the architectural style of the Swabian castles in Puglia and Sicily. It was built at the order of Frederick II between 1237 and 1247 over the remains of an earlier manor of the counts of Prato.

CHURCH OF SANTA MARIA DELLE CARCERI – With a Greek cross plan, the building was designed by Giuliano da Sangallo (1484-95). The interior is considered a masterpiece of Renaissance architecture for the harmonious arrangement of space and the perfect balance of layout.

CIVIC MUSEUM – Created in 1858 and housed in the rooms of **Palazzo Pretorio** (13th-14th centuries), the museum has various important collections, mainly of the Florentine school from the 14th to 15th centuries. Just some of the numerous works of importance here are: the *St Margaret Tabernacle* by Filippino Lippi (1498); a predella with *Seven Episodes of the*

Holy Girdle attributed to Bernardo Daddi; *Virgin and Child with Saints* by Bernardo Daddi (1328); *Virgin Enthroned with Child and Saints* by Giovanni da Milano (1354); the famous *Madonna del Ceppo* by Filippo Lippi (1452).

MUSEO DELL'OPERA DEL DUOMO – The museum is located in the **Bishop's Palace** (Palazzo Vescovile) beside the cathedral and amongst the works exhibited is the *Death of St Jerome* by Filippino Lippi (1452).

TEXTILE MUSEUM

Located in the former Campolmi factory this museum provides an interesting overview of textile production in the period from the 15th to the 19th century.
Exhibited are many fine and rare fabrics from the collection donated by Loriano Bertini.

CENTRE OF CONTEMPORARY ART

The Luigi Pecci Centre for Contemporary Art came into being in 1988 as a result of the initiative of an industrialist from Prato, Enrico Pecci. Its creation was a highly important event on the Italian artistic scene as it was one of the few museums specifically dedicated to contemporary visual arts. The architectural structure was designed by Italo Gamberini. Located near to the industrial area, it is surrounded by important works of sculpture by artists such as Enzo Cucchi, Mauro Staccioli and Anee and Patrick Poirier who made the gigantic Fallen Column of steel with a quote from Horace in Latin that states, "I raised a monument more lasting than bronze". The exhibition area now consists of three specific departments: Exhibitions, Permanent Collections, Culture. First and foremost an exhibition centre, shows concentrate mainly on artistic production over the last ten years, but also of the post-war period. The permanent collections contain works of various movements, such as conceptual art, 'arte povera' and the 'transavanguardia' including both the most famous names as well as younger and more recent arrivals on the Italian and international artistic scene. The centre hosts seminars, conferences, films, plays, multimedia performances and concerts as well as publishing and offering a didactic and school service.

The castle of Cafaggiolo (above) and the villa of Poggio a Caiano (left).

THE MEDICI VILLAS

Situated around Florence are some stupendous villas which still bear witness to the power held by the Medici family. The buildings are quite magnificent in style and yet architecturally are sombre and imposing.

The **Medici villa at Poggio a Caiano** (1480), for example, was built by Giuliano da Sangallo for Lorenzo il Magnifico. It is composed of two wings linked by a large reception hall, while a beautiful portico with pillars surrounds the building and a sweeping stairway leads to the first floor. The interior is decorated with a series of 16th-century frescoes.

Villa Demidoff originally had a 16th-century layout but is now quite different in appearance. Some works of art are still located in the park, such as the *Colossus of the Apennines*, a gigantic statue made by Giambologna between 1579 and 1580.

Villa La Petraia, once a medieval tower belonging to the Brunelleschi family, was transformed into a residence for the Medici by Bernardo Buontalenti. Some important frescoes by Volterrano are inside. The beautiful garden has a *fountain* by Tribolo and a bronze *sculpture* by Giambologna.

The **Medici Villa at Careggi** was already the property of the Medici in 1417 and was enlarged by Michelozzo in 1457.

The **Medici Villa at Castello**, now the headquarters of the *Accademia della Crusca* (the academy of the Italian language), was built in the sturdy style of the 15th century. The interior is decorated with frescoes by Pontormo and Volterrano.

The **Medici castle at Cafaggiolo** was one of Lorenzo de' Medici's favourite residences. It was built in the mid 15th century over a 14th century fortified structure and is located in the Mugello, the area from which the Medici family originated. A masterpiece of Renaissance art, it was designed by Michelozzo.

PISTOIA

The earliest inhabitants were probably Etruscans. In Roman times Pistoia (Pistorium or Pistoriae) became a Roman municipality.

Its greatest development was in the 2nd-3rd century AD, when it was made a diocese. It was conquered by the Goths and then, for a brief period, by the Byzantines. Subsequently, under the Lombards, Pistoia's prestige began to grow and it became an administrative centre. In the 11th century it became a free commune and in 1177 promulgated its own statute, one of the oldest in Italy. During the 12th and 13th centuries the city experienced considerable economic, cultural and artistic growth. Following two disastrous defeats by Florence in 1228 and 1254 it came under Florentine rule.

CATHEDRAL – The earliest record of a church dates from the 10th century. Between the 12th and 13th centuries it was altered several times in the Pisan Romanesque style. The beautiful **façade** has three orders of loggias and a spacious porch with an important bas-relief in glazed terracotta by Andrea della Robbia in the vault. The tripartite **interior** contains a shrine with the remains of the *sarcophagus of St Matthew* with three bas relief panels attributed to Agostino di Giovanni (1337); in the right nave is a beautiful wooden crucifix by Coppo di Marcovaldo (1275); beyond is the **Chapel of St Jacob** with the Saint's magnificent *silver altar*, one of the finest works of Italian silverwork, produced by Andrea di Jacopo d'Ognabene, Leonardo di Giovanni, Nofri di Buto and Atto di Piero Braccini. Another excellent work of art is the *Madonna Enthroned with Child and Saints* by Lorenzo di Credi (1485), probably made from a design by Verrocchio.
The ancient **Romanesque crypt** is entered from the church and housed here is the *Monument to Cardinal Niccolò Fonteguerri* (1419-1473), a composite work by Verrocchio, Lorenzo di Credi and Lorenzetto, and the lovely *baptismal font* by Andrea Ferrucci da Fiesole, deigned by Benedetto da Maiano.

BAPTISTERY - A small octagonal building in black and green marble built to a design by Andrea Pisano in the first half of the 14th century.

PALAZZO COMUNALE – Dated late 13th century, the building houses the **Civic Museum**, where important works dating from the 13th to the 16th centuries are exhibited,

The dome of the Madonna dell'Umiltà church stands out in this view of roof tops in Pistoia.

including a painting of St Francis in the Pisan style (13th century), one of the oldest works of art remaining in Pistoia; a wooden crucifix by Salerno di Coppo (1275) and the remains of some 13th century frescoes.

BISHOP'S PALACE – The palace is 11th century and houses the **Cathedral Museum** where reliquaries and religious furnishings are displayed. Of particular interest are the highly refined *Chalice* and the *Cross of Sant'Atto* (second half 13th century); *St Jacob's Reliquary* made by the workshop of Lorenzo Ghiberti about 1407; the *Reliquary of the Virgin*, another fine example of the art of the goldsmith in the late Middle Ages. The museum also has a collection of archaeological artefacts from the urban area.

CHURCH OF SANT'ANDREA – Built in the 13th century on an ancient earlier foundation (8th century), this church is a perfect gem of Pistoian architecture. The interior has three naves and contains the renowned *Pulpit* of Giovanni Pisano (1301) and a wooden *Crucifix* also attributed to him.

SPEDALE DEL CEPPO – Situated in Piazza San Giovanni, along the façade of this building dating from the 13th to 14th centuries, is the famous frieze of enamelled terracotta (16th century) portraying the *Seven Works of Mercy*. The first six panels are by Giovanni della Robbia and Michele Viviani; the other is by Paladini. Beneath the frieze are five medallions and half medallions with garlands of fruit and flowers by Giovanni della Robbia, representing the most significant *Marine Episodes*. Ancient doctor's instruments once used in the hospital are the rather unusual exhibits in the **Museum of Surgical Instruments** located here.

Above: the pulpit by Giovanni Pisano in the church of Sant'Andrea and one of the glazed terracottas that decorate the façade of the Spedale del Ceppo.

Below: the Palazzo Comunale in Pistoia (left) and the façade of the Spedale del Ceppo (right).

The spa in Montecatini.

MONTECATINI TERME

The city lies in a broad plain at the end of the Val di Nièvole. It is famous for its spas and the spring water is prevalently of sulphate-alkaline water, an authentic cure-all for disorders of the liver and the digestive apparatus. The springs in this area were already known in ancient times but it was only at the beginning of the 1900s that they became of interest on a national and European level and today's spa complex developed. Many of the establishments are in neoclassic and Art-nouveau style and it is well worth a visit to see the **Excelsior, Leopold Spa, Tamerici, Regina, Tettuccio, Torrette, Rinfresco, La Salute** and **Redi** buildings.

COLLODI

This ancient village (late 12th century) lies on the slopes of a hill near Pescia. Nearby are many splendid estates, including **Villa Forti** in Chiari and **Villa Cecchi**, known as the *Guardatoia*, but the finest of all is the imposing **Villa Garzoni** (now Gardi dell'Ardenghesca), built between 1633 and 1662 on the site of a medieval castle in a baroque style typical to Lucca. Behind the villa lies the town of Collodi whose fame is in part due to the fact that the Florentine writer Carlo Lorenzini (1826-90), the author of *Pinocchio*, used the name as his pseudonym. He passed his childhood here in the town where his mother was born. In its labyrinth of lanes, Collodi retains a medieval character, clustered around the **church** that was founded in the 14th century and the ruins of the **keep**.

Not far from Villa Garzoni, near the **Osteria del Gambero Rosso**, designed by Giovanni Michelucci in 1963, is the **Park of Pinocchio** with the *monument to Pinocchio and the Fairy* by Emilio Greco (1956), the **Piazzetta dei Mosaici** by Venturino Venturi and the **Paese dei Balocchi** (Land of Toys) where Pinocchio's adventures are enacted.

Two sculptures in the Pinocchio Park in Collodi.

CHIANTI

Situated between Florence and Siena there is a third city, known as Chianti. This third city is formed of castles, fortresses, towers, towns, farms, Romanesque churches, rectories and chapels.

Extending from the river Arno in the north to the Ombrone in the south, thus between the two centres of Florence and Siena, the exact Chianti region is formed by a vast expanse of attractive gentle hills alternating with occasional areas of bare limestone, crossed by deep river valleys that, here and there, have created small flood plains (such as, for example, those made by the rivers Greve, Pesa and Elsa). The countryside is partly agricultural and partly wooded, verdant and skilfully cultivated by centuries of labour.

This light, open landscape is perfectly bordered by soft slopes and the undulating profile of hills and mountains such as the delightful Chianti hills, reaching their greatest height with Monte San Michele (893 metres), and then extending down to the red hills of Siena and further on to the lunar landscape of the 'crete'. Today, Chianti covers about 70,000 hectares. Two thirds of this is still covered in oak woods, as well as chestnut trees and conifers, where boar, hares, deer and pheasants live; the soil of the entire area drains over stone and rock and is therefore clean and dry, well suited to the cultivation of vines and olives. Long ago that Tuscan miracle known as Chianti wine originated here, and with that same name appeared in documents as early as the 14th century. Traditionally the boundaries of Chianti coincide with those of the area of wine production and consequently, on the whole, the limitations established in a grand ducal proclamation of 1716 are still respected today.

THE WINE HARVEST

Grape harvesting in the countryside became a real wine festival, with great suppers prepared by the labourers' families followed by parties and dancing. It took days to gather the bunches of grapes and separate the wine grapes from those to be used for the Vin Santo, which were left to dry on rush mats raised on a structure of sticks.

Modern-day tourists who generally have little time to spare but many interests to satisfy can choose between culture, visits to museums, excursions in the countryside, shopping at farms, village fairs – there are as many different ways to enjoy the region as there are reasons for its popularity.

TOWNS AND AREAS TO VISIT

San Casciano Val di Pesa, Tavarnelle Val di Pesa, Castellina in Chianti, Gaiole in Chianti, Radda in Chianti, Greve in Chianti, San Gimignano, Panzano, San Miniato, Montalcino, Buonconvento, Colle Val d'Elsa, Monteriggioni, Volterra

CHIANTI DOCG

The Chianti Consortium was formed by the wine producers of the provinces of Arezzo, Florence and Siena and today has some 2000 producers of Chianti Classico, the finest of all the Chianti wines. In fact, two Consortia actually exist, the "Consorzio di Marchio Storico" (Historic Brand) and the "Vino Chianti Classico"; the former has the task of promoting the brand in Italy and abroad while the latter is responsible for inspecting and protecting the designation.

The Chianti DOCG (appellation controllée e garantée) is now produced in an area covering the provinces of Siena, Florence, Arezzo, Pistoia, Prato and Pisa. The basic grapes of Chianti production are Sangiovese (75-100%), Canaiolo (up to 10%), Trebbiano and Malvasia (up to 10% and up to 6% for 'Classico'), with the addition of red grapes to a limit of 10% and of 15% for 'Classico'. The wine of Chianti is ruby red in colour, tending towards a garnet shade with age, and has a harmonious, dry and full flavour which is slightly tannic, with an intense perfume similar to that of violets.

Some Chiantis can be drunk young when the wine is fresh and pleasant to the palate, but other areas are known and appreciated for their improvement with medium to long-term aging which matures the singular colour, perfume and flavour.

The wine harvest.

The Chianti countryside with its gentle hills covered with vines.

GREVE IN CHIANTI

The town lies around its large and unmistakable triangular piazza where a market has always been held and where a monument has been placed to Giovanni da Verrazzano, the intrepid sailor and discoverer of the bay where New York was founded, who was born in 1485 nearby in the Castle of Verrazzano. Also facing onto this piazza is the interesting **church of Santa Croce**. Beside the little church of San Francesco, in the old Franciscan monastery, is an important **Museum of Sacred Art**. Nearby, both the elegant **Uzzano Castle** and the little **San Cresci church**, one of the oldest in Chianti, are well worth a visit.

The porticoed piazza of Greve in Chianti (below) where the statue of Giovanni da Verrazzano stands (above) and a statue by the contemporary sculptor, Mitoraj (right).

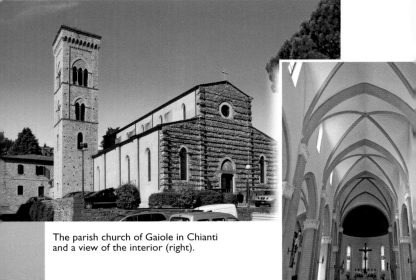

The parish church of Gaiole in Chianti and a view of the interior (right).

GAIOLE IN CHIANTI

The town of Gaiole came into being in an area where reminders (as well as names and ruins) of the Etruscans and Romans still abound and has developed around a triangular piazza surrounded by shops and workshops. The immediate area is still steeped in a fascinating medieval atmosphere that is present in the important religious buildings, noble manor houses and fortified settlements that were all part of the widespread feudal system created by the Firidolfi, ancestors of the Ricasoli family.

CASTELLINA IN CHIANTI

The town developed on the site of one of the oldest Etruscan settlements and was destroyed in the 14th century by the troops of the Duke of Milan, an ally of Siena. The Florentines subsequently built a new ring of *walls* and

THE STORY OF THE BLACK COCKEREL

Legend has it that the first "gallo nero" in the history of the Chianti hills was in fact of the genuine feathered kind. In the Middle Ages the ruling powers of Florence and Siena reached an agreement for an equal division of the Chianti territories.

On an agreed day, at first cockcrow a horseman would leave at a gallop from each city, racing in the direction of the other. The border between the possessions of the two States would be fixed at the point where the two riders met.

The tower of the keep overlooks
Castellina in Chianti.

fortifications, most of which have survived, including a **stronghold** where the town council is now located.

In addition to the parish church of **San Salvatore**, where an interesting detached fresco of the *Virgin and Child* by the Maestro di Signa is housed, **Palazzo Ugolini** (16th century) is a fine, elegant building.

Castellina in Chianti is, however, particularly noted for its exceptional urban structure preserved almost intact within its walls with a network of streets, alleys and arches, typically rural **houses** dating from the 15th-16th centuries, and the fascinating, ancient **Via delle Volte**.

RADDA IN CHIANTI

Between the Arbia and Pesa valleys, this ancient castle was a military outpost of Siena until 1176 and then fell under the jurisdiction of Florence. Recognising its vital strategic importance in dominating this more distant area of Chianti, Florence assured the town's development by declaring it the foremost town of the *Lega del Chianti* and creating an extensive system of fortifications (14th -15th centuries). The new defensive walls enclosed the town with the severe **Palazzo del Podestà** at its centre. The old Franciscan convent of **Santa Maria al Prato**, now housing the Museum of Sacred Art, is also of interest. Nearby the **Poggio La Croce archaeological site**, datable to the first millennium BC, indicates that a stable settlement has existed in the area since ancient times.

General view of Radda in Chianti.

SIENA

On the softly rolling hills of the countryside between the valleys of the Arbia, the Elsa and the Merse lies Siena.

The earliest detailed information dates from the Roman period. We, know, for instance, that Siena, at the time Sena Julia, must have been a Roman civitas (legend maintains that the city was founded by Aschio and Senio, Remus' two sons). After the Carolingian conquest it was governed by the Bishops until the 11th century when it became a free commune. This was when the city experienced its first great period of territorial and urban expansion, thanks to the flourishing commerce and trade which depended on the route followed by the Via Francigena, linking the city to the area north of the Alps. In the 12th and 13th centuries the city, by now rich and powerful, often clashed with the neighbouring city of Florence on which it inflicted a crushing defeat in 1260 in the famous battle of Montaperti. Many outstanding personalities were also born during this period such as Duccio da Buoninsegna, Simone Martini and Ambrogio Lorenzetti who influenced the entire 14th century with their artistic masterpieces. In 1269 the Sienese were drastically defeated at Colle Val d'Elsa, this time by the Florentine troops, and a period of decline set in.

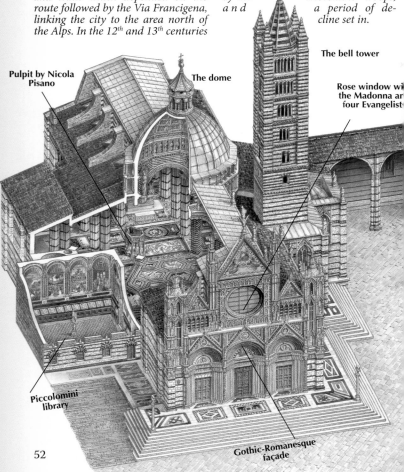

Pulpit by Nicola Pisano

The dome

The bell tower

Rose window with the Madonna and four Evangelists

Piccolomini library

Gothic-Romanesque façade

Siena became a signoria in 1487, and in the 16th century it allied itself with the French and in 1559 surrendered to the troops of Giangiacomo de' Medici thus passing under the dominion of Cosimo 1. In the centuries that followed it was governed by the Lorraine family and in 1859 it was the first Tuscan city to be annexed to the Kingdom of Italy.

Stained glass window in the apse of Siena cathedral, designed by Duccio di Buoninsegna.

CATHEDRAL - Construction began towards the end of the 12th century but before the mid 14th century work on the Cathedral came to a halt and it was planned instead to create a church of such a size that the existing building would have served merely as its transept. Lando di Pie-

View of Siena cathedral.

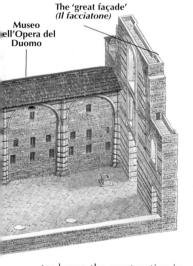

The 'great façade' (*Il facciatone*)

Museo ell'Opera del Duomo

tro began the construction in 1339, but the ambitious project was abandoned in 1355. The Cathedral of Siena houses an incredible number of works of art. The **façade**, for example, is decorated with Giovanni Pisano's statues, made around 1290 and now replaced with copies, while the originals

are in the city's Museo del Opera. The most striking feature of the **interior** is the marble pavement, decorated in sgraffiti or intarsia made between the mid 13th century and the mid 16th century. Artists such as Domenico di Niccolò and Domenico Beccafumi worked on the inlays. The circular stained glass window in the apse with stories of the *Virgin, Evangelists* and *Patron Saints of Siena* was made in the late 13th century from designs by Duccio di Buoninsegna and is probably the oldest stained glass decoration made in Italy. In the left transept, near the area covered by the dome, is the famous octagonal *pulpit* by Nicola Pisano with *Events from the Life of Christ* and made with the help of his son Giovanni and Arnolfo di Cambio.

Interior of the cathedral.

Other fine works here are the *tomb stone* of Bishop Giovanni Pecci, a bronze by Donatello, and the **Chapel of St. John the Baptist** with a bronze *Baptist* by Donatello and the **Chapel of the Madonna del Voto** (or **Chigi Chapel**), financed by Alexander VII shortly after the middle of the 17ᵗʰ century, and designed by Bernini.

Opening off the left nave is the **Libreria Piccolomini**, founded towards the end of the 15ᵗʰ century by cardinal Francesco Todeschini Piccolomini (the future pope Pius III) and frescoed by Pinturicchio.

To the right of the cathedral is the abandoned extension of the **New Ca-**

Duccio di Buoninsegna's *Maestà* in the Museo del Opera.

thedral where the **Museo del Opera Metropolitana** is now housed.

THE BAPTISTERY OF SAN GIOVANNI - Building started on the Baptistery in 1316. The façade, made towards the end of that century, has remained incomplete and is traditionally attributed to Giacomo di Mino del Pelliccaio. The **interior** has a *baptismal font* by Jacopo della Quercia. The sculptural decorations are by Renaissance masters and include works by Ghiberti and Donatello.

MUSEO DELL'OPERA METROPOLITANA - Created in the later 19ᵗʰ century, this museum contains mainly works of art that were once in the cathedral. The *ten statues* by Giovanni Pisano that decorated the cathedral façade until the 1950s are housed here, as is a small *wooden crucifix*. A relief sculpture portraying the *Virgin and Child, St Jerome and Patrons*, made by Jacopo della Quercia for the altar of Cardinal Casini in the cathedral, was dismantled and remounted in the museum. The most important work in the museum is the *Maestà* by Duccio di Buoninsegna which enhanced the main cathedral altar until 1505. Dating from the first decade of the 14ᵗʰ century, this work signalled the beginning of a magnificent period in Sienese painting. The *Madonna and Child* from the Church of Santa Cecilia at Crevole is an early work by Duccio. The tryptych of the *Birth of the Virgin* is a mature work by Ambrogio Lorenzetti, signed and dated 1342 by him. Also displayed in the museum is a splendid work by Simone Martini, the *Blessed Agostino Novello* dated around 1130. The cathedral's illuminated manuscripts and some rare items from the Treasury are also housed in the museum.

PIAZZA DEL CAMPO

PIAZZA DEL CAMPO - This famous sloping shell-shaped piazza came into being in the mid 12th century when the public authorities began to acquire the land where it lies. A fine and harmonious feature of the piazza is the **Fonte Gaia**, decorated with sculptures by Jacopo Della Quercia, the originals of which are now located in Palazzo Pubblico.

PALAZZO PUBBLICO - An integral part of Piazza del Campo, the Palazzo Pubblico was created as an extension of an earlier building following the demand for a single location for the city authorities in 1282, though work continued until the mid 15th century. Work then began on building the **Torre del Mangia**, constructed by Minuccio and Francesco di Rinaldo, though Lippo Memmi was responsible for designing the top section. The **Cappella di Piazza**, begun in 1352 by Domenico di Agostino though completed by Giovanni di Cecco, was built at the bottom of the tower to fulfil a vow made during the plague of 1348.

Taking its name from the map, since lost, once painted in this room by Ambrogio Lorenzetti, the **Sala del Mappamondo** with the *Maestà* (1315) and *Guidoriccio da Fogliano* by Simone Martini, are all worth a visit inside the Palazzo.

The **Sala dei Nove**, which was the seat of city government, is famous for the frescoes by Ambrogio Lorenzetti, the most extensive series of paintings portraying a secular subject dating from the Middle Ages. In

Palazzo Pubblico seen from the air (above) and from Piazza del Campo (right).

The 'Mangia' Tower

Capella di Piazza

San Bernardino rosette

the *Effects of Good Government* Lorenzetti provides not only an allegorical image, but also a view of the city and its countryside that is one of the most important representations of the environment and everyday life inside the city and in the country. Directly opposite this, the fresco of the *Effects of Bad Government* is sadly much damaged.

Also in the Palazzo is the **Civic Museum** with objects of the minor arts, coins, seals and more paintings. In the wing of the Palazzo near to the Torre della Mangia is the delightful **Cortile del Podestà,** built in the 1330s but restored just before 1930. In the courtyard is the entrance to the **Teatro Comunale dei Rinnovati** which was originally the hall of the Grand Council of the Republic until 1560.

SIENESE GOTHIC

During the late 13th century Sienese art reached its apex with Duccio di Boninsegna. The compositional elegance and decorative subtlety of Sienese Gothic differentiated it from Florentine medieval painting. In Duccio's *Maestà* (1309-1311) Byzantine and Gothic influences combine to produce one of his most sublime works. This magnificent moment of Sienese Gothic continued with masterpieces by Simone Martini such as the *Maestà* (1317), frescoed in Palazzo Pubblico. Simone soon became one of the most popular painters in the capitals of Gothic art from Naples to the papal court in Avignon. Another Gothic artist was Piero Lorenzetti whose later masterpiece (1342) the *Birth of the Virgin*, is

exhibited in the Museo dell'Opera Metropolitana. His works reflect the influence of Giotto in the volume of the forms and the sombre modulation of the composition. The largest medieval cycle of secular paintings, where the Gothic spirit is most fully expressed with the representation of life and exaltation of the new civic ruling class, was the work of Pietro's brother, Ambrogio Lorenzetti who painted the *Effects of Good and Bad Government in the Town and the Countryside* in Palazzo Pubblico (1337-39). Tino di Camaino, a pupil of Giovanni Pisano, was an important Sienese Gothic sculptor who combined the linear rigour of his master with the forms and movement of classical tradition.

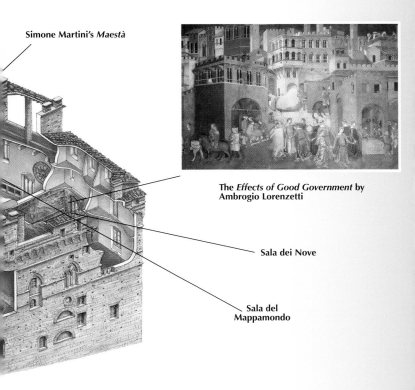

Simone Martini's *Maestà*

The *Effects of Good Government* by Ambrogio Lorenzetti

Sala dei Nove

Sala del Mappamondo

The Fonte Gaia in Piazza del Campo, a copy of the original by Jacopo della Quercia, the remains of which are now in the loggia of Palazzo Pubblico.

The start of the Palio and the flag bearers.

THE PALIO

Every year the Palio takes place in the Piazza del Campo on 2 July and on 16 August. In its present form the race dates back to the first half of the 15th century, even though a less spectacular version was run in Siena as early as the 13th century. The event represents an annual renewal of the ancient rivalries between the various districts of the city. Siena is divided into 17 districts, each of them named after a real or imaginary animal: Aquila (eagle), Chiocciola (snail), Onda (wave), Panther (panther), Selva (rhinoceros and oak), Tartuca (tortoise), Civetta (owl), Leocorno (unicorn), Nicchio (ocean shell), Torre (elephant with tower), Valdimontone (rampant ram), Bruco (caterpillar), Drago (dragon), Giraffa (giraffe), Istrice (porcupine), Lupa (wolf), Oca (goose). A procession takes place before the Palio and precedes the arrival of the ten horses and jockeys who will vie in the competition, seven districts having been excluded in each race by drawing lots. The horses are lined up near a rope, known as "canapo" and when it is lowered they streak off to circle the piazza three times. The course is

Images of the Palio.

almost circular and downhill in stretches and is far from easy for the horses and their riders, but the prize at stake is high and at the end the winner will be carried in triumph and celebrated for days on end.

PINACOTECA NAZIONALE

Sienese painting from its origins to the mid 17th century is exhibited in the National Gallery, located in Palazzo Buonsignori since 1930. The most important work by Duccio, the great innovator of Sienese painting, is the *Madonna dei Francescani*. The *Madonna and Child* from the church of Lucignano d'Arbia is one of Simone Martini's greatest works. The *Madonna and Child with Saints, Doctors of the Church and Angels* is by Ambrogio Lorenzetti, as is the *Annunciation* signed and dated 1344. His brother, Pietro Lorenzetti, was a rather more dramatic artist and works by him include the *Madonna and Child with Saints* and the *Stories of the Carmelite Order*, once part of the large altarpiece painted by Pietro in 1328-29 for the Carmine church in Siena, later dismantled. The *Last Supper* and *St Anthony possessed by Devils* are by Stefano di Giovanni, known as Il Sassetta.

One of the most important Sienese artists during the 15th century was Lorenzo di Pietro, better known as Il Vecchietta, who was both a painter and sculptor. *St Catherine receiving the Stigmata*, the *Birth of the Virgin* and *Christ in Limbo* are all works by Beccafumi (Domenico di Jacopo di Pace), perhaps the greatest Sienese painter of the 16th century.

The *Madonna dei Francescani* by Duccio di Buoninsegna in the National Gallery.

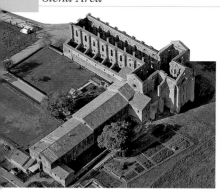

Aerial view of the Abbey of San Galgano.

Apse of the church of San Galgano.

THE ABBEY OF SAN GALGANO

The Abbey was one of the most important examples for the diffusion of the Gothic Cistercian style in Italy. The **church**, with a Latin cross plan, was built by the Cistercians between 1224 and 1288. The structure was partially ruined in the 18th century by the collapse of the vaulted roof and the bell tower. The incomplete façade has four columns and three semicircular arches. Beside the church is the **Monastery** of which only the **Chapter House** and **Monks' Hall** with two aisles formed by pillars remain. On the upper floor a narrow corridor leads to the monks' **cells** and the choir.

Abbey of Sant'Antimo.

THE ABBEY OF SANT'ANTIMO

It is traditionally believed that the Abbey of Sant'Antimo, which was one of the richest and most powerful in Tuscany, was founded by Charlemagne. The monastery is almost completely ruined and today only the massive proportions of the **church** with its 12th-century bell tower remain as evidence of former grandeur. The **bishop's apartments**, built in the former women's' gallery on the right in the church are probably early 13th century. The decorative sculpture is of exceptional quality, especially the carving of the capitals, and the author of the capital carved with *Daniel in the Lion's Den* has been identified as the 'Master of Cabestany'.

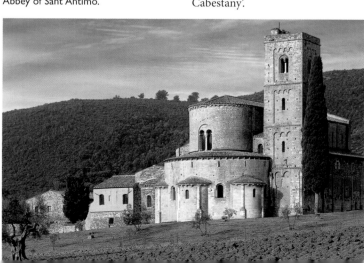

COLLE DI VAL D'ELSA

The town developed at the centre of an area that was already settled in Etruscan and Roman times; in the 13th century it became an independent commune, but in the middle of the 14th century passed under the dominion of Florence and with the decline of Siena's power, experienced a period of peace and economic prosperity. The urban structure of the historic centre of Colle consists of an upper part (**Colle Alta**) formed by **Castello** and **Borgo** and an area that developed lower down (**Colle Bassa**).

The Castle is on the eastern and steeper side of the hill and the main square, the **Palazzo Pretorio**, **Palazzo Comunale** and **Cathedral** are here.

The cathedral, constructed on the site of an ancient church, is an elegant late mannerist building designed by Fausto Bugliesi from Montepulciano, while the façade was made at the beginning of the 19th century.

The bronze *lectern* was made by Tacca and a *crucifix*, also in bronze, is by Giambologna. The marble *pulpit*, dated 1465 is possibly by Benedetto da Maiano. The **Cappella del Chiodo**, where a relic of the Holy Cross is housed, is also of interest. Further to the east, a robust **tower house** is traditionally believed to have been the home of Arnolfo di Cambio.

Borgo di Santa Caterina is a natural extension from the Castello area along the crest of the hill towards the west. It is mainly located on the continuation of the street that ends at the Renaissance **Porta Nova** (or **Volterrana Gate**) attributed to Giuliano da Sangallo.

In **Colle Bassa**, only the **Porta Guelfa** and the southern side of the defensive walls that protected the lower part of the town now remain. The **Sant'Agostino** and the **San Francesco** monasteries are of considerable interest.

Colle di Val d'Elsa.

Colle has interesting collections of works of art in various small museums: the **Civic Museum**, the **Museum of Sacred Art** and the **Bianchi-Bandinelli Archaeological Museum** located in the Palazzo Pretorio, a collection of items from various Etruscan tombs in the surrounding area dating from the 7th century BC to the Roman period. Also on display here is a **permanent exhibition** regarding the works of **Arnolfo di Cambio**, Colle Val d'Elsa's most famous historic figure.

View of Montalcino and the fort.

MONTALCINO

Montalcino's **Rocca**, or Fortress, begun in 1361 by Mino Foresi and Domenico di Feo, has the form of a walled castle with a pentagonal layout of which three sides are perpendicular, and with towers at each corner. Inside, at the northern tower, are the remains of the **Castle Chapel**. In front of the towers facing south is an extensive **bastion** built during the Medici period. On the lower side of the town little remains of the **walls** though a lengthy section still exists on the side opposite.

Piazza del Popolo - This square represents the centre of the town and facing onto it are a 14th-15th century **Loggia** and the **Palazzo Comunale**, originally the **Priors'** palace.

"Musei Riuniti", Church of Sant'Agostino - The **Archaeological Museum** has prehistoric and Etruscan items from the surrounding area, but in particular from the *Tomb of the Treasury* near Sant'Angelo in Colle (3rd century BC) and the *Sant'Antimo Hollow*.

The **Civic and Diocesan Museum** has a 12th-13th century painted *Crucifix* from Sant'Antimo, one of the oldest painted works from the Sienese territory. Also of interest are the polychrome *wood statues* by Francesco di Valdambrino and the 14th-15th century *maiolica* made in Montalcino, one of the oldest centres for the production of ceramics in Tuscany. The fine illuminated *Bibbia Atlantica* dated second half of the 12th century, is from the Abbey of Sant'Antimo.

MONTEPULCIANO

The town was already inhabited in the Etruscan period and was claimed by both Florence and Siena until in 1208 it became an independent commune. Following various events it finally came under the jurisdiction of the Medici.

Cathedral – Designed by Ippolito Scalza, it was built between 1592 and 1630. The **bell tower** dates from the later 15th century. It houses a painting of *Saint Sebastian* by a pupil of Andrea del Sarto and in the first chapel (now the **baptistery**) is the *Annunciation with Four Saints*, a glazed terracotta work by the school of Andrea della Robbia.

Church of Sant'Agostino – Designed by Michelozzo, there is also a terracotta relief of the *Madonna with Saints John and Augustine* over the entrance. The most important works of the **interior** are the prestigious *Madonna della Cintola* by Barocci, the *Raising of Lazarus* by Alessandro Allori, a *Crucifixion* with the Virgin and Mary Magdalene by Lorenzo di Credi.

Palazzo Comunale - Dating from the later 14th century, the façade appears to be the work of Michelozzo. Inside is a lovely **courtyard**. The palazzo faces onto Piazza Grande, looking not unlike a stage set surrounded by austere palaces and enhanced by the *pozzo de' Grifi e de' Leoni* (Griffins and Lions Well), a delightful Renaissance piece.

Civic Museum – Located in Palazzo Neri Orselli, the museum houses many important works including two glazed terracotta *altar pieces* by Andrea della Robbia, a *Madonna and Child* by the school of Duccio di Buoninsegna, a captivating *portrait of a woman* by Spagnoletto, portraits by Sustermans, Paris Bordone and Santi di Tito, as well as works by Filippino Lippi and Cigoli.

Church of Santa Lucia – Various important works are found here, such as the *Madonna della Misericordia*, a masterpiece by Luca Signorelli, and a *wood crucifix* by G. B. Alessi.

View of Montepulciano.

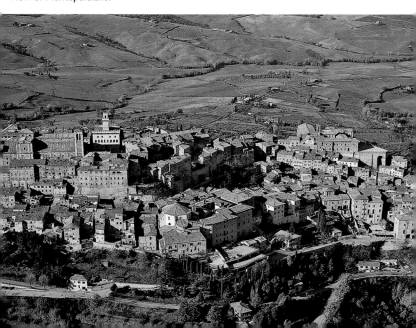

The fortified village of Monteriggioni.

MONTERIGGIONI

Situated on the top of a small hill, the village of Monteriggioni is entirely surrounded by a magnificent circle of walls from which rise fourteen rectangular **towers**. The village was built by the Sienese in 1203 as an outpost against the Florentines and due to this vulnerable position it continually passed from the dominion of one to the other. The walls were built between 1213 and 1219 and cover a distance of about 570 metres enclosing this tiny but delightful hamlet which includes an intimate little parish **church** in Romanesque-gothic style.

Monteriggioni's parish church.

PIENZA

In 1458, cardinal Enea Silvio Piccolomini became Pope and took the name Pius II. In just a few years the town of Castello di Corsignano, where Pius II had been born and spent his childhood years, not only entirely changed its urban layout but also assumed the status of township on becoming a bishop's see. Complete restructuring of Castello began in 1459 under the direction of the pope's architect, Bernardo Gambarelli da Settignano, better known as "Il Rossellino". On becoming a township, the original name was changed to Pienza.

The centre provides a unique example of 15th century urban organization, built according to precise urban concepts derived from the ideal city conceived on the basis of Humanist precepts.

Piazza Pio II – the centre of the town and a true Renaissance gem, the Cathedral, Bishop's Palace, the Canon's House and Palazzo Piccolomini all face onto this square.

The **Cathedral**, dedicated to the Virgin, is Rossellino's greatest achievement. Below the presbytery is a **crypt** with an elegant baptismal font designed by Rossellino, and fragments of Romanesque sculpture that decorated the old church of St Mary. Just two of the cathedral's works of art are the *Assumption of the Virgin* by Vecchietta and a *marble altar with silver reliquary*, probably by Bernardo Rossellino.

The **Bishop's Palace** was built by Cardinal Rodrigo Borgia, later Pope Alexander VI, in the 15th century.

The **Cathedral Museum** is located in the **Canon's House** (Casa dei Canonici) and houses works of art from the cathedral and other churches in the diocese of Pienza. Important works of art here include an elaborate *pastoral* in gilded silver donated to the cathedral by Pius II and the famous 14th century English *cope* that belonged to him, a gift from Thomas Paleologus. Lastly, cinerary urns, amphora, goblets and other material from excavations of Etruscan and Roman sites is displayed in a small annex.

The **Piccolomini Palace** is Rossellino's masterpiece with an internal courtyard from which one reaches the **Hanging Garden** with a magnificent view over the Val d'Orcia. The elegance of the 15th century continues in the **interior** of the palace and is evident in the furnishings, the coffered wooden ceilings, the library and fine collections of weapons, musical instruments and artistic items.

THE PECORINO OF PIENZA

Highly appreciated by Pius II himself, this particular type of pecorino cheese is made in the area of the Sienese 'crete' from the milk of sheep that graze freely feeding on herbs with a strong aromatic flavour which emerges in the cheese itself. Shaped like a flattened round, pecorino matures for over two months, becoming crumbly in texture with a slightly spicy flavour, though still preserving the smoothness it has when young and fresh. The skin is typically rough and uneven, red if treated with oil and tomato, brown if treated with oil and ash. Traditionally it is eaten together with walnuts and pears.

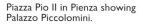

Piazza Pio II in Pienza showing Palazzo Piccolomini.

SAN GIMIGNANO

The town of San Gimignano came into being in the centre of an area which was already inhabited in the Etruscan and Roman periods and became an independent commune in 1130. The 13th century brought a period of economic expansion and it was at this time that the wealthier families built those towers that are still a remarkable feature characterising the landscape. During the 14th century the influence of Florence in-creased until the town finally submitted in 1353. Three gates of the oldest ring of walls (11th century) still exist. The second ring is almost complete extending east and westwards to include the settlements that stood on the Via Francigena. The towers and houses that have made San Gimignano so famous are concentrated around **Piazza del Duomo** and **Piazza della Cisterna**, forming the centre of the town. The most notable

Above and below, views of San Gimignano.

are the **Torre Grosso del Palazzo del Popolo**, the **Rognoso** and the **Cugnanesi** towers, the twin towers **Ardinghelli** and **Salvucci**, the **Cortesi** (or **Devil's**) tower.

Palazzo del Podestà and Palazzo del Popolo – The ancient **Palazzo del Podestà**, rebuilt in 1239 and enlarged one hundred years later, stands beside the Rognoso tower. A **theatre** was built inside the palace. Opposite is the **Palazzo del Popolo** (now the town hall) with its tower, the highest of all in San Gimignano, standing on the right. A plaque on the Palazzo records that Dante Alighieri stayed here when he came to plead the cause of the League of the Guelfs. The rooms where once the town magistrates met, now house the **Civic Museum** and **Gallery**. In the Museum is the *Maestà* which Lippo Memmi painted in 1317, clearly inspired by Simone Martini's work painted two years earlier in the Palazzo Pubblico in Siena. The Gallery also has a fine collection of paintings of the Sienese and Florentine schools from the 13th to the 15th centuries including, for example two tondos with the Annunciation by Filippino Lippi.

The Collegiata – Also incorrectly known as the cathedral, is the old parish church of San Gimignano, consecrated in 1148 by pope Eugene III. As early as the 14th century, the **interior** of the church was decorated with frescoes by artists such as Taddeo di Bartolo, Barna da Siena, Lippo Memmi, Bartolo di Fredi, and more were added after enlargement in the 15th century. Benozzo Gozzoli, Domenico Ghirlandaio, Pier Francesco Fiorentino and Sebastiano Mainardi all worked on the large fresco cycles of the 15th century. The church also has wood sculptures by Jacopo della Quercia.

Other works and religious furnishings of considerable quality are now housed in the **Museum of Sacred Art** located together with the church archives (**Archivio Capitolare e dell'Opera**) in the little Piazza Pecori.

The well dated 1287 which stands in the middle of the square named after it.

Piazza del Duomo in San Gimignano.

THE LAND OF BRUNELLO

The area of Montalcino is famous not only for its artistic masterpieces and historic towns and monuments, but also for its superior wine, Brunello, recognised as one of the best in the entire world. The history of this wine, aged in oak for 4 or 5 years at least, starts with Ferruccio Biondi Santi, a stubborn yet far-sighted Tuscan, a 19th-century gentleman farmer and rival of Bettino Ricasoli, "inventor" of Chianti wine. But while the "Baron of Brolio" based the original structure of Chianti on a mixture of red and white grapes, the father of Brunello decided to attempt a pure vinification using only a Sangiovese grape (the "Sangiovese Grosso") in the hope of obtaining a superior wine that would have a long life. And he was proved right. His son Tancredi standardised Brunello and introduced it to the market, achieving in just a few decades enviable praise and approval.

Barrels of Brunello di Montalcino.

MURLO

BUONCO

MO

ROSSO DI MONTEPULCIANO

The wine of Montepulciano is a deep ruby red colour with a dry, harmonious and slightly tannic flavour. As a young wine, served at about 18°, it is a good all-rounder, particularly suited to pasta dishes with meat sauce, white meats, poultry as well as beans, salame that is not too spicy and youngish cheeses. With aging it is a good accompaniment to red meats, both roast and grilled.

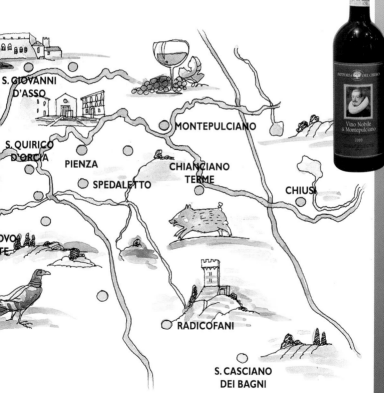

S. GIOVANNI D'ASSO

S. QUIRICO D'ORCIA

PIENZA

SPEDALETTO

MONTEPULCIANO

CHIANCIANO TERME

CHIUSI

RADICOFANI

S. CASCIANO DEI BAGNI

AREZZO

Arezzo is situated at the confluence of four fertile valleys: the Casentino, the Valdichiana, the upper Valdarno, and the upper part of the Valtiberina.

It was with the arrival of the Etruscans that Arezzo rapidly became a flourishing and powerful centre, to such an extent that, with the other most important Etruscan cities of the time, it even promised aid to the Latins against the king of Rome, Tarquinius Priscus. Under Roman rule it continued to prosper until the 1st-2nd century AD when as a result of interminable internecine struggles a rapid decline set in. In 575 it fell under Lombard rule and then passed to the Franks until it became part of the Marchesate of Tuscany. In the 11th century it became a free commune and about this time the city rivalled Florence for supremacy over the region until it was finally irremediably defeated by the Florentines in the battle of Campaldino (1289). Arezzo thus fell under the Florentine sphere of influence and subsequently became part of the Grand Duchy of Tuscany.

THE MEDICI FORTRESS – Built in the 16th century by Antonio and Giuliano Sangallo, this is a robust star shaped fortification with bastions. From the terraces there is a magnificent view sweeping as far as Pratomagno and the Catenaia alps.

CATHEDRAL AND DIOCESAN MUSEUM - Building began at the end of the 14th century. The façade is recent (1901-1914) and was designed by Dante Viviani. The **interior** has three naves without a transept. The magnificent stained-glass windows are by Guillaume de Marcillat. Particularly interesting at the end of the right nave is the **Cappella Tarlati** (1334). Near the entrance to the sacristy is a famous fresco of *Mary Magdalene* by Piero della Francesca, and on the left is the imposing *cenotaph of Guido Tarlati,* completed by

Aerial view of Piazza Grande in Arezzo.

Agostino di Giovanni and Agnolo Ventura, probably to a design by Giotto. On the left nave is the '**Madonna del Conforto' Chapel** dating from the late 18th century and housing fine works such as the terracotta *Assunta* by Andrea della Robbia, the *Crucifix with saints Donatus and Francis*, also by Della Robbia, and a *Madonna and Child* by his workshop. Important works originally in the cathedral and other churches of the diocese are exhibited in the adjacent **Museo Diocesano**.

CHURCH OF SAN DOMENICO - The church was built after 1275 and was probably designed by Nicola Pisano. The Gothic-style **bell tower** stands to the side of the façade. In the **interior** are some excellent works of art, such as the famous Crucifix, an early work by Cimabue.

CHURCH OF SAN FRANCESCO - Originally built in the 13th century, though the existing structure is a 14th century adaptation. Built in brick and stone, the style is Tuscan and Umbrian Gothic. As is usual in Franciscan architecture, the **interior** consists of a single large nave at the end

THE CHIMERA OF AREZZO

The Chimera, symbol of the city of Arezzo, represents the mythological monster which had a lion's body and three heads. It was found in Arezzo in 1553 and is now exhibited in the Archaeological Museum of Florence. The bronze sculpture dates from the 5th-4th century BC and was probably part of a votive group with Bellerophon, now missing. During restoration in the 18th century the tail in the form of a serpent was added. The monster was represented in various ways and the Arezzo Chimera probably was inspired by Homer's description in the Iliad, "She had the head of a lion and the tail of a serpent, while her body was that of a goat, and she breathed forth flames of fire" (Iliad VI, 223-225).

Piero della Francesca
Sansepolcro 1420 - 1492

Constantine's dream

One of the twelve episodes of the famous fresco cycle dedicated to the *Legend of the True Cross* and now restored. Before his victory over Maxentius in the Battle of Milvian Bridge near Rome, Constantine sees the cross in a dream. Legend has it that it appeared to him with the words "By this sign you shall conquer " and the next morning the emperor ordered the *labarum* to be made – a standard that replaced the Roman eagle with the monogram of Christ's name at the top and under which the soldiers were to fight. Labaro is the name of a Roman village on the Via Flaminia and probably the place where Constantine succeeded in putting his enemy to flight, giving chase as far as the Milvian Bridge. The Roman Emperor thus converted to the new religion and the following year, in 313, he issued the Edict of Milan giving Christians the right to worship freely.

Palazzo Pretorio.

PALAZZO PRETORIO - Many medieval and renaissance sculptures are housed in this building which is now the city's **library** with over 80,000 volumes including incunabula, 16th century books and illuminated manuscripts.

VASARI'S HOUSE, MUSEUM AND ARCHIVE - The house and museum is entirely decorated with fine frescoes, many by Vasari himself, and represents late 16th-century Tuscan taste and style. Works exhibited in the **Camera di Apollo** include a *St Francis* by Alessandro Allori and *St Jerome* by Jacopo Ligozzi. Also housed in the Gallery is a famous *Christ in Judgement* by Fra' Bartolomeo.

ROMAN AMPHITHEATRE AND MECENATE ARCHAEOLOGICAL MUSEUM - Part of the seating and side aisles of the **amphitheatre** remain. Located in the 16th-century **Monastery of St Bernard**, the **Archaeological Museum** has remains dating from prehistory to the Roman era, and in particular from the Etruscan period including a valuable collection of sealed ceramic jars (1st century BC - 1st century AD).

The Vasari Loggia in Piazza Grande.

of which are three square chapels. A large **crypt** extends beneath the nave. There are many important works in the interior, but the best known is the splendid fresco cycle in the choir, the *Legend of the True Cross* by Piero della Francesca made between 1453 and 1464. Now completely restored, this is one of the most important works of the entire 15th century.

CHURCH OF SANTA MARIA - Built between the 12th and 14th centuries this parish church is one of the most important Romanesque buildings in the region. The delightful façade clearly shows the influence of Pisan Romanesque and the **bell tower**, nicknamed "cento bocche" (one hundred mouths) for its numerous windows and mullions, dates from the 14th century. The **interior** has three naves and a trussed roof. At the end is the **crypt** over which the presbytery is built.

PALAZZO DEI PRIORI - Built in 1333, it is now the seat of the city council. Alongside stands the robust **medieval tower** (1337). In the **Council Chamber** is an interesting *portrait of Pietro Aretino* which has been attributed to Sebastiano del Piombo.

MUSEUM OF MEDIEVAL AND MODERN ART - The museum is situated in the old **Palazzo Bruni-Ciochi**. The paintings exhibited span a period of time from the 13th to the 19th centuries. Some of the most famous works here are *St Francis in Ecstasy* by Margaritone d'Arezzo, a magnificent *Madonna della Misericordia* by Bernardo Rossellino, *Virgin with Saints and Angels* probably by Luca Signorelli, and the *Adoration*, also by Signorelli. Also on display is an excellent collection of maiolica dating from the 13th to 18th centuries.

THE JOUST OF THE QUINTAIN

Surrounded by an attractive series of palaces and tower-houses, Piazza Grande is noted for its unusual disposition which is irregular and

disproportionate on the upper side. A game of jousting in historical costume is held in the piazza, an ancient tradition that dates from the Middle Ages, but was reinstated in 1930. Twice a year on the penultimate Saturday of June and first Sunday in September the city's four districts compete in the joust. The quintain (a large wooden figure with a metal shield attached to the left arm and a long flail with three lead balls covered with leather on the right arm) is located in the north-east corner of the piazza. Each district is represented by a horseman who has to strike the shield with his lance, while avoiding being hit by the speedily rotating flail.

THE ANTIQUES FAIR

Since 1968, stalls of antiques fill Piazza Grande when the Arezzo Antique Fair is held on the first weekend of every month. With some 500 exhibitors from all over Italy it attracts as many as 20-30,000 visitors on each occasion. The first event of its kind in Italy, it was initiated by Ivan Bruschi, an important collector and antiquarian from Arezzo. The Ivan Bruschi Museum, with his collection of over 10,000 items, is now housed in the 14th-century Palazzo del Capitano del Popolo.

ANGHIARI

Situated in a lovely hilly area, the newer part of the town is below, while the old part is perched above on a high slope. The **Museum of Popular Crafts and Traditions of the Upper Tevere Valley**, located in the Taglieschi Palace, contains sculptures and detached frescoes from the churches of Anghiari and the Tevere Valley. Amongst the famous artists exhibited are the Della Robbia, Antonio Sogliani, Jacopo Vignali and Matteo Rosselli.

Palazzo comunale in Cortona.

CAPRESE

On the slopes of the Catenaia Alps lies the old village of Caprese Michelangelo, famous as the birthplace of the great artist born here on 6 March 1475. Places of interest here are the **Buonarroti house and museum**, the **church of St John the Baptist** and the remains of a **14th century castle**.

THE BATTLE OF ANGHIARI

The battle took place on 29 June 1440 between the forces of Florence and Milan. It lasted an entire day and at the end there was only one victim who died as a result of a fall from his horse. The battle is, however, of note thanks to the famous competition between Leonardo and Michelangelo for the decoration of the walls of the Salone dei Cinquecento in Palazzo Vecchio in Florence. In 1503 Leonardo was commissioned to portray Florence's victory at Anghiari, and Michelangelo the battle of Cascina. Neither of them completed their work, though Leonardo did transfer part of the preparatory sketches to the wall. The little that he did succeed in achieving provided a superb model that was copied by many painters until it was covered over by Vasari's new decoration in 1563. The Museum of the Battle of Anghiari in the Marzocco Palace documents the battle and exhibits reproductions of Leonardo's preparatory drawings and a reconstruction of the fresco.

CORTONA

Already renowned in the Etruscan period, Cortona became an ally of Rome in the 4th century BC. In the first centuries of the first millennium it was taken by the Goths. In the 13th century it became a free commune but in the late 1200s it was occupied by Arezzo. The town subsequently became a signoria of the Casali family. In 1411 it entered the Florentine sphere of influence and then followed the destiny of the Grand Duchy of Tuscany. The **Cathedral**, probably built on the remains of the earlier church of Santa Maria, was designed and built by the great Giuliano da Sangallo.

Interesting works of art include a lovely *Madonna and Saints* by Cigoli, a *Crucifixion* and *St Thomas* by the school of Signorelli, and *Madonna and Saints* by Alessandro Allori. The cathedral, probably built on the remains of the earlier church of Santa Maria, was designed and built by the great Giuliano da Sangallo. The **bell tower** has two storeys with mullioned windows and was built in 1566 by Francesco Laparelli. With its simple linear façade and fine portal the **church of San Francesco** dates to the first half of the 13th century. The interior contains fine works of art including a beautiful painting of *St Anthony of Padua* by Cigoli and a touching *Annunciation* by Pietro da Cortona.

Palazzo Comunale is an imposing building dating to the first half of the 13th century. Inside, the **Sala del Consiglio** is a delightful room.

An important collection of Etruscan, Roman and Egyptian artefacts is located in the **Museo dell'Accademia Etrusca** in **Palazzo Pretorio**. The museum also houses numerous paintings and examples of the applied arts dating from the 13th to the 19th centuries. Paintings are by such artists as Niccolò di Pietro Gerini, Pinturicchio, Ghirlandaio, Bicci di Lorenzo, Piazzetta, Pietro da Cortona, Jacopo da Empoli and Alessandro Allori.

Situated opposite the cathedral in the old **Chiesa del Gesù** is the **Diocesan Museum**. The collection contains works of considerable interest, especially of the Tuscan school. Most important of all however, is the renowned and beautiful *Annunciation* by Fra' Angelico, one of the artist's best loved works. In addition there is a large wood *crucifix* by Pietro Lorenzetti, a *Madonna and Child with Four Saints* also by Fra' Angelico, a *Madonna and Child* by the school of Duccio da Buoninsegna, as well as other works by Lorenzetti, Sassetta, Signorelli and Giuseppe Maria Crespi.

The **Medici Fortress**, also known as the **Girifalco Fortress**, dominates the city from the top of the hill. It was built in 1556 by Gabrio Serbelloni and is now used for exhibitions and cultural events.

ETRUSCAN NECROPOLI

Below Cortona are various tombs of the Etruscan period. Two of these are known as the **'Melone di Camucia'** (7th century BC) and the **'Melone del Sodo'** dating from the same period.

Originally an Etruscan hypogeum, the **'Tanella di Pitagora'** probably dates from the 4th century BC and has a barrel vault beneath which six burial niches would have held cinerary urns.

The sanctuary at La Verna.

LA VERNA

Since the 13th century this has been one of the most important centres of the Franciscan order. This rocky peak, donated to St Francis by Count Orlando dei Cattani was a wild and lonely place until in 1215, Francis of Assisi built the first humble huts of mud and woven branches for himself and his followers. The saint became particularly fond of the spot and in 1224 it was here that he received the stigmata. A flourishing Monastery of the Order of Minorites is still located in La Verna and the village has become a large complex of buildings. The 14th century church of **Santa Maria degli Angeli** is immediately inside the Sanctuary and contains two altars with glazed terracotta works by Giovanni della

Robbia. The *Madonna della Cintola* (1486) by Andrea della Robbia is on the high altar. Various other works by the Della Robbia and their workshop are also found in the **Chiesa Maggiore**, or **Church of Santa Maria Assunta**.

The portico around the Chiesa Maggiore continues, becoming the **Corridor of the Stigmata** leading to the **Chapel of the Stigmata** where there is a large glazed terracotta altar panel representing the Crucifixion, by Andrea della Robbia and, over the door a *Madonna and Child* by Luca Della Robbia. The Monastery itself consists of several buildings, including the **guest lodge**, the **refectory**, **dormitory** and **library**.

SANSEPOLCRO

It is traditionally believed that the town developed around an oratory dedicated to St Leonard which contained relics of the Holy Sepulchre. The historic centre still has an unspoilt urban structure and plan dating from the 15th-16th centuries.

In the **Cathedral**, dating from the first half of the 11th century, are several important works of art, including the beautiful *Assunta* by Palma il Giovane, and the *Volto Santo*, a wood sculpture of the Carolingian period, earlier than, and perhaps also the model for, the more famous *Volto Santo* in the cathedral of Lucca.

Exhibited in the **Civic Museum**, located in the Palazzo della Residenza, are many works of great artistic interest: the famous fresco of the *Resurrection* and the *polyptych of the Madonna della Misericordia*, both masterpieces by Piero della Francesca; *Saints Egidio and Anthony,* a fine work by Luca Signorelli; the *Pietà* and *Saint Nicholas of Tolentino* are both by Santi di Tito; works by Raffaellino del Colle, Agostino Ciampelli, the Della Robbia, Cigoli and Passignano.

The **Church of San Lorenzo**, built in 1556, has a lovely façade with a portico. A *Deposition* by Rosso Fiorentino is inside and represents one of the most famous paintings of the Mannerist period.

The **Medici Fortress**, probably built by Giuliano da Sangallo, is a fine example of a 16th-century military building.

The town has many fine buildings some of the most interesting being the **Palazzo delle Laudi**, built at the end of the 16th century and now the seat of the town council, **Palazzo Pretorio** the façade of which is decorated with coats of arms made by the Della Robbia, and **Palazzo Graziani** built in the 16th century and much influenced by Ammannati.

THE "MADONNA DEL PARTO" IN MONTERCHI

It is well worth taking the time to visit the small medieval town of Monterchi near Sansepolcro where, in a chapel by the cemetery, one of **Piero della Francesca**'s finest works, the *Madonna del Parto*, is located. This great artist was born in Sansepolcro and other famous paintings by him are found there, such as the Resurrection, which has become a symbol of the town. In 1467 he painted this powerful image of the Virgin shown in the late months of her pregnancy with the Son of God. Perhaps Piero had his own mother, born in Monterchi, in mind when he painted this fresco. Clothed in a dress with a front opening, as was worn by pregnant women at the time, the natural pose is balanced by the strong symbolism of the image with its dome-like form, a shrine revealed to the observer by the two symmetrical angels opening the curtains on either side.

CAMALDOLI, POPPI, AND CASENTINO FORESTS

The Casentino area has always provided a suitable location for the monastic and hermetic life. Thus in the heart of these ancient woods of beech and fir, designated a National Park in 1993, important centres of the Christian faith have been established, such as La Verna and Camaldoli. The religious complex of Camaldoli consists of the **Fontebuona Monastery**, which came into being for pilgrims, and the **Hermitage** for the monks and was the first home of the order created in 1023 by Romuald. The town of Poppi is in the Casentino as is the Castle of the Conti Guidibuilt in the 13th century to a design that is reminiscent of Palazzo Vecchio in Florence. The **Chapel** on the second floor is frescoed with **Stories of the Life of Christ and John the Baptist**, attributed to Taddeo Gaddi. The sweeping panorama from the tower of the castle, across Bibbiena and the valley below, is quite magnificent.

THE ARCHERY COMPETITION

Held on the second Sunday of September every year, in honour of Sant'Egidio, the centuries old traditional archery competition recreates the flavour and atmosphere of olden days.
Reliable sources indicate that it already took place in 1300. The competition is an age-old challenge against the town of Gubbio and is now preceded by flag throwers and followed by a procession in historical dress. Every item of both the men's and women's clothing is a faithful reproduction of models taken from the frescoes of Piero della Francesca. The game itself is quite simple: the arrow ("veretta") has to strike the centre of the target (the "cherry" or "yew") which is placed at the far side of a playing field.

General view of Poppi.

GROSSETO

Grosseto lies in the heart of the Maremma, near the right bank of the Ombrone river which winds its way across this vast plain.

This prevalently modern city has spread out around the small compact historical centre marked by the old Medici bastions. In 1138 Innocent II transferred the cathedral from Roselle, which had declined, and from then on, Grosseto continued to develop into a small city. It became a free commune but following a series of events, in 1336 it fell to the Sienese. In 1559 it came under the dominion of the Medici who, while they restricted its freedom, also helped it to prosper, initiating a programme of land reclamation (centuries of malaria had seriously depleted the population of the area around Grosseto) and building the magnificent walls that surrounded and protected the city.

CATHEDRAL - Begun in 1294 and completed early in the 14th century. There is a fine *baptismal font* by Antonio Ghini (1470) inside and a splendid *Assumption* (15th century) by Matteo di Giovanni.

MUSEO ARCHEOLOGICO E D'ARTE DELLA MAREMMA (ART AND ARCHAEOLOGICAL MUSEUM) - The **prehistoric section** is installed on the ground floor with material from the Palaeolithic to the Villanovan periods. The **Etruscan section** presents material from the excavations of ancient settlements including Talamone, Vetulonia, Cosa, Sovana, Castro, Vulci, Pitigliano, Saturnia, Magliano and above all Roselle. There is also a rich **collection of religious art** on the second floor. Paintings of the Sienese school dating from the 13th to the 17th centuries include in particular the famous *Madonna of the Cherries* by Sassetta, as well as a fine collection of ceramics.

CHURCH OF SAN FRANCESCO - An austere 13th-century building in Gothic style. The convent buildings are on the left side. Still extant is a **Cloister** with the *well* nicknamed the "bufala", built by Ferdinando I towards the end of the 16th century. Inside the church is a valuable *cross* set behind the high altar, perhaps an early work by Duccio da Buoninsegna (1289).

MEDICI WALLS AND FORTRESS - The bastions that completely enclose the historic centre of Grosseto are hexagonal in form. Grand Duke Francesco I ordered them to be made and they were designed by Baldassare Lanci (1574). In 1835 the terraces and ramparts were transformed into public gardens and at one corner of the walls rises the **Medici Fortress** which incorporates the old Sienese Keep.

Grosseto cathedral.

Grosseto, palace housing the provincial administration.

Cathedral of Massa Marittima.

ANSEDONIA

Known as Cosa in Roman times, the town of Ansedonia dominates the landscape of the lagoon of Orbetello and Monte Argentario. The ruins of ancient Cosa consist of the **capitolium**, the **acropolis**, **temples**, **forum** and other buildings. Destroyed by the Barbarians and rebuilt in the late Middle Ages, during the 10th century Ansedonia was frequently raided by Saracen pirates and was finally taken by the Sienese. Near to the **Spacco della Regina**, a natural cleft in the rock, is the **Torre della Tagliata** where Giacomo Puccini once lived.

MASSA MARITTIMA

This delightful town is probably of Etruscan origin but only became an important centre in the 9th century when it was chosen to be a bishop's seat. In 935 it was almost completely destroyed by the Saracens. In the Middle Ages it was one of the most flourishing free communes, thanks to the exploitation of copper and silver mines nearby. Frequently in conflict with both Florence and Siena, it was defeated by the Sienese in 1335. In 1555 it came under the dominion of the Medici.

Cathedral - This lovely building in Romanesque style dates from the first half of the 13th century.
The **interior** has three naves; at the

beginning of the nave on the right is the **Baptistery**, with a rectangular font engraved with the *Life of John the Baptist* by Giroldo da Como (1267). In the **Chapel of the Crucifix** is a beautiful *wood crucifix* by Segna di Buonaventura and in the left transept is a magnificent panel painting of the *Madonna delle Grazie* made in 1216 by Duccio di Buoninsegna or follower. The *reliquary of San Cerbone*, a 14th century Sienese piece and a reliquary *cross* with silver leaf by Meo and Gaddo Andreassi (15th century) are in the **Chapel of the Reliquaries**. The famous *Arca di San Cerbone*, a splendid Sienese Gothic sculpture made by Goro di Gregorio in 1324, is housed below the apse.

Palazzo Pretorio - This solid austere building in travertine dates to the first half of the 13th century. The two upper floors are enhanced by a row of two-light windows which enliven and illuminate the structure. Once the residence of the Podestà, today the Palazzo Pretorio houses public offices as well as the **Archaeological Museum** where interesting items from Etruscan tombs are exhibited.

Palazzo Comunale - The building, which dates to the 13th-14th century, is actually the result of the fusion of several medieval tower-houses. The central section of the palazzo is instead an original construction designed by Stefano di Meo and Gualtiero del Sozzo (14th century). On the right, the part known as the **Torre del Bargello** dates from the early 13th century. The interior of the Palazzo Comunale is decorated with numerous frescoes.

Museum of Sacred Art - Opened in 2005, the museum houses works of art from the area around Massa. The works can mainly be identified as Sienese and Pisan art, the two areas most involved in the history of the town. The beautiful *Maestà* by Ambrogio Lorenzetti alone makes a visit to the museum worthwhile.

ORBETELLO

The town is at the centre of the lagoon of Orbetello, which is about 27 square kilometres, from which two strips of sand known as *tomboli* emerge. An artificial dam, built in 1842, joins it to the promontory of the **Argentario**. A visit to Orbetello may begin at the **Porta *Medina Coeli***, which was part of the old circuit of walls. The gate leads into Piazza Quattro Novembre, surrounded by the **Spanish fortifications**. The **Palazzo della Pretura** houses the **Antiquarium**, a museum with archaeological material from

Etruscan and Roman times discovered in the surrounding territory. Particular attention should be paid to the archaic *sphinx* of the 7th-6th century BC, various amphorae and finely made sculptures.

THE MUSEUM OF MINING OF MASSA MARITTIMA

Built in second world war anti-aircraft shelters, the Museum of Mining recreates a real mine with excavations of seven hundred metres, three tunnels and six hundred working tools. The various types of equipment used to support the vaults of the galleries and the different techniques used to work the seams and deposits are all reproduced and explained in this underground environment.
The Museum of the Art and History of Mining is located in the 15th-century Palazzetto delle Armi. On display are many photographs and maps, mining tools used from antiquity to the 20th century, as well as a collection of minerals and everyday items used by the miners.

View of Orbetello in the centre of its lagoon.

THE MAREMMA

The area extends from southern Tuscany as far as north-western Lazio and is divided into **Maremma pisana** (north of Piombino) and **Maremma grossetana** (further south). Towards the interior it stretches over the western slopes of the Colline Metallifere for a total area of around 5000 square kilometres. Along the beautiful coast are many well-known sea resorts such as **San Vincenzo**, **Follonica**, **Marina di Grosseto**, **Punta Ala**, **Castiglion della Pescaia** and **Porto Santo Stefano**.

This isolated area was for centuries badly infected by malaria. It was only with an immense programme of land reclamation, begun in 1828 by Leopoldo II, Grand Duke of Tuscany, and later permanent re-utilization at the beginning of the 20th century, that the Maremma has become entirely habitable and productive.

The figure of the **Buttero** is a characteristic and traditional feature typical of this area. His job is to drive herds of cattle along difficult and tortuous roads, brand the various herds of cattle and break in the famous and ancient breed of native Maremma horses. Part of this territory is now the **Natural Park of the Maremma** (also known as the **Uccellina Park**) where a variety of important ecosystems ranging from the hills to the sea form the unspoilt landscape. Further north, in the area between Viareggio

Above, **herdsman** on horseback in the Maremma. Below, a herd grazing.

and Livorno, the **Natural Park of Migliarino**, **San Rossore** and **Massaciuccoli** includes woods, undeveloped coastal areas, farm estates, rivers, lakes, marsh and agricultural land. The different kinds of terrain with their varying microclimates have given rise to habitats suitable for a great variety of animals.

Scenes at the **Merca**, a springtime event, held for branding the herds.

SEA RESORTS IN THE MAREMMA

Follonica,
Punta Ala,
Castiglion della Pescaia,
Marina di Grosseto, Talamone,
Porto Santo Stefano.

THE LAGOON OF ORBETELLO AND THE NATURE RESERVE

The area around the Giannella 'Tombolo', or sandbar, joining the coast of the Maremma to the Argentario promontory forms the Regional Nature Reserve of Orbetello. Extending over some 1,553 hectares situated within the territory of the local Commune, the area also includes the **Patanella Wood** and the **Casa Giannella** area which represents the "State Nature Reserve for Animal Population", managed by the Italian WWF. Numerous animals, not normally seen around the coasts of Tuscany, are to be found here, such as sea eagles, flamingos, grebes, ducks, coots, cormorants, egrets, spoonbills, harriers and stilt plovers.

Beyond the Lagoon of Orbetello rises the Argentario headland. Located in this undulating landscape are important seaside resorts such as Porto Santo Stefano and Porto Ercole, which has impressive 16th century walls around an interesting historic centre. At Cala Galera, near to Porto Ercole, Caravaggio died on 18 July 1610.

THE UCCELLINA PARK

Named the **Maremma Park** when it was founded, but now more familiarly known as the Uccellina Park, this protected area stretches for just under nine thousand hectares from the mouth of the river Ombrone on the north, to the Talamone point in the south, and covers the territories of Grosseto, Magliano and Orbetello. The park incorporates the **Palude della Trappola** which is one of the most interesting marsh environments in Tuscany where horses are still raised in an almost wild state and Maremma cattle are bred. The **Uccellina Hills** also lie within the park, high grounds that are covered with trees and shrubs typical of the Mediterranean 'macchia'. The long coastal strip alternates stretches of limestone rock where the sea is inaccessible, and small bays and larger inlets, such as the lovely **Cala di Forno**, just to the south of **Piana di Portovecchio**, once a landing place for smugglers and now an exclusive small harbour. Areas where the vegetation is thicker are havens for wildlife such as boars, deer, porcupines, badgers and martens.

Damper parts give shelter to mallards, wild geese, teals and lapwings. Flying between sea and land are the seagulls, tireless guardians of the park, while the numerous watch towers and the **Abbey of San Rabano** are the only man-made, "unnatural" elements in this corner of paradise on earth.

An intriguing view of Pitigliano.

PITIGLIANO

This charming village is a gem amongst those built of tufa in this region. It was ruled by Vulci in Etruscan times, and later by the Romans, and in the Middle Ages belonged to the Aldobrandeschi and Orsini.

The **Cathedral**, dedicated to Saints Peter and Paul, was rebuilt between the 16th and 18th centuries, though it was originally medieval. The arches of the 16th century **aqueduct** stretch from the 16th century **Fortress** to the impressive **Palazzo Orsini**, built between the 14th and 16th centuries. It is probable that Giuliano da Sangallo and Peruzzi collaborated on the construction.

SATURNIA

This small town lies surrounded by a ring of walls built by the Sienese in 1461 on what was left of the preceding walls, thought to be Etruscan.

The **Porta Romana** towers over a paved street of the Roman period. Etruscan and Roman antiquities are exhibited in **Villa Ciacci** where remains of the old Sienese keep are visible.

The town is known mostly for the **springs** here. The hot springs of Etruria are today an exceptionally important natural and therapeutic resource, not only due to the sulphurous waters at a temperature of 37° C. generally recognised for their many curative qualities, but also for the environmental aspect of the wonderful hot waterfall that attracts numerous visitors. It is certain that the Etruscans already knew the health-giving properties of the water in this area and most probably made use of them. In Roman times the whole area of Etruria was famous for its therapeutic waters. A visit to the **Etruscan necropolis** just a few kilometres from Saturnia is most rewarding.

Hot water springs at Saturnia.

View of the village of Vetulonia.

SOVANA

The great quantity of burial grounds in the surrounding area is evidence of the extent of the Etruscan civilization (3rd century BC). In the Middle Ages Sovana was noted for being the birthplace of Pope Gregory VII (Hildebrand of Sovana). From the 14th century it was ruled by Siena.
Bordering the picturesque **Piazza del Pretorio** are various interesting medieval buildings: **Palazzo Pretorio** (13th century) with its **Loggetta del Capitano**; **Palazzo Bourbon del Monte** (16th century); the **Palazzo dell'Archivio** (12th-13th centuries); the **church of Santa Maria** dating from the 13th century.
The **cathedral**, built before 1000 AD, was influenced by the Lombard-Romanesque style. In the interior is the 15th-century Sarcophagus of St Maximilian. The **Aldobrandesco Fortress** stands just outside the walls.

THE ARCHAEOLOGICAL PARK OF THE 'TUFA' CITY

Just outside the village of Sovana is a vast necropolis cut out of the rock.. Tombs of various periods and kinds are found here, such as the **'Sirena' Tomb** (Mermaid) of the 3rd-2nd centuries BC, and the **Tifone Tomb** (2nd century BC). The famous **Hildebrand Tomb**, dated 3rd-2nd centuries BC, is named after Hildebrand of Sovana, who became Pope in 1073 with the name of Gregory VII and tradition maintains that he was buried here. Completely cut into the tufa rock of the hillside, the sepulchre consists of two parts: the underground chamber itself and the monument above, shaped like a small temple. The oldest necropoli are **Poggio Stanziale** and **Sopraripa**, dating from the 7th-6th

The Hildebrand tomb, a large Etruscan burial place in the Sovana necropolis.

centuries BC. There are numerous deep Etruscan roads dug into the tufa rock in the area.

ROSELLE

Standing just a few kilometres from Grosseto, the excavations of the Etruscan and Roman city of Roselle are open to the public. The town is surrounded by a **circuit of walls** over three kilometres long, which has been miraculously preserved in its entirety from the 6th century BC. In the heart of the Roman city is the **Forum**, with broad streets of volcanic stone, on either side of which are the most important public buildings, such as the **Basilica** with rectangular ground plan and portico, used for the administration of justice. The paving in stone slabs of the Forum of Roman Imperial times still exists opposite. Further south is what is thought to have been the **seat of the *Augustales***, a room with niches in the walls, which contained marble statues of the emperor *Claudius*, *Livia* and other personages of the Julio-Claudian dynasty. On the slopes of the north hill, not far from the road that leads to the excavations, are the **Roman baths** with mosaic pavements and the base of a **medieval tower**, while near the top of the hill are other **Etruscan buildings** of the archaic period and the **Roman amphitheatre** of the first century AD. On the south hill, excavation has brought to light a vast inhabited centre with streets, houses and artisans' workshops of the late 6th century BC, above which lies a later urban settlement of the Hellenistic period. Unlike the town, the necropoli of Roselle have never been studied in detail despite the fact that the burial chambers were discovered in the 19th century and many important furnishings and articles found there have confirmed that the area was flourishing, in particular between the 6th and 5th centuries BC. Many of the tombs are burial chambers covered with slabs, datable to the late 7th – early 6th century BC.

Aerial view of the necropoli at Roselle.

The excavations at Roselle.

THE VETULONIA NECROPOLIS

The extensive necropoli are all that is left to provide us with a precise idea of the wealth and power of this centre, which developed from the 8th century BC on when the copper, silver, and lead mines in the Colline Metallifere began to be exploited. The tombs of the archaic period, situated in the heights surrounding the city (Poggio alla Guardia, Colle Baroncio, Poggio alle Birbe, etc.) have rendered many objects in decorated bronze and locally made gold and silver jewellery, as well as precious handmade objects imported from the eastern Mediterranean area, Phoenicia and Egypt as well as Sardinia. Frequent trade and contact with the Etruscan cities of northern Lazio brought exotic products to Vetulonia as can be seen from the quality of the items found in the 'Circolo' tombs,

probably built for the burial of members of the same family. Some of the richest of these tombs are the **'Circoli' dei Monil**i, **Bes**, the **Pellicce**, the **Lebeti**, the **Trident**, and the **Tomb of the Duke**, dating to the late 8th- mid-7th century BC. In the second half of the 7th century BC, the monumental tumulus tombs of the nobility make their appearance, with square chambers and false vaulting supported by a central pier: two superb examples along the **Via dei Sepolcri** are the **Tomb of the Pietrera** and the **Tomb of the Diavolino**. The following centuries have not left many traces, but a few recent finds seem to indicate that life in Vetulonia continued uninterrupted throughout the 6th and 5th centuries BC, blossoming into a new period of prosperity in the 3rd century BC.

Terracotta antefix

Bronze buckle

Gold pin

THE ETRUSCANS IN THE MAREMMA

Stable occupation of the area dates from the early iron age and can be explained by the presence here of both forests and minerals, and by the particular conformation of both the coasts and interior. Small clusters of villages gradually developed into small cities by exploiting the potential of local resources, thus creating an important flow of trade crossing Etruria during the 7th century BC. But it was as sea-faring cities that they really flourished, for at the time the coast of the Maremma had many more inlets than it does today. In addition to the large **Baratti Gulf**, which is still a magnificent protected expanse of water, there used to be a vast internal marine lagoon, the **Prile Lake**, onto which both Roselle and Vetulonia faced. This area has now been reclaimed and is part of the Grosseto Plain.

Maritime links with the island of Elba and the other coastal cities of Etruscan Lazio are witnessed by finds relating to trade. From these it can be deduced that these cities flourished as long as the Etruscans maintained their supremacy over the seas, until, that is, about 474 BC, when they were defeated by the Syracuse fleet in the waters of Cumae. Some of the cities made a comeback between the 4th and 3rd centuries BC under Roman influence. The founding in 273 B.C. of Cosa, a Roman colony to be used as port of call, led in fact to the further decline of some of the ports and heralded the gradual Romanization of the area. With the fall of the Roman empire, the Maremma underwent a relentless decline and became greatly depopulated.

Ceramic vases

Waste from ironworks

Funerary urn with sloping cover

THE PORTUS COSANUS AND THE TAGLIATA ETRUSCA

The "Tagliata Etrusca" is an impressive example of Roman engineering which, together with the "Spacco della Regina", a deep natural cleft in the rock, facilitated the ebb and flow of the sea to avoid the silting up of the ancient harbour of Cosa. In ancient times the old *Portus Cosanus*, was situated here, at the base of the Ansedonia headland on the steep eastern coast, and remains of it are still visible in the sea.

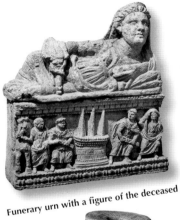

Funerary urn with a figure of the deceased

Ceramic jugs

The Etruscan "tagliata".

LIVORNO

Just a few kilometres from the mouth of the River Arno, Livorno is one of Italy's major sea ports.

The origins of the city are rather uncertain, but in any case it is in recent times that the city has come into its own. After Pisa fell to the Florentines (1405), Livorno passed under Genoa which a few years later ceded it to Florence for 100,000 florins. On 28 March 1577 the foundation stone of modern Livorno was laid when it was decided to build a new port there as the old port of nearby Pisa was by now completely silted up. This was the beginning of the city's prosperity; the population quadrupled and it rapidly became an extremely important maritime centre. With the building of the great Medicean port it became a crossroads for vital international trade in the 17th and 18th centuries. During the Second World War the city was heavily bombed and some of its most important monuments were destroyed.

One of the *Four Moors*

MODIGLIANI AND MASCAGNI

In the 19th and 20th centuries, Livorno was the birthplace of several important personalities. The Museum of Villa Mimbelli, for example, is dedicated to Giovanni Fattori, while another great artist of the late 19th-early 20th centuries was Amedeo Modigliani, born here in 1884, who left the city as a young man to travel to Florence, Venice and then Paris. The Museo Mascagni, in the annex of Villa Maria, is dedicated to the great musician who was born in Livorno in 1863. Mementos, photographs, manuscripts and scores relating to his life and work are exhibited here.

The Old Fortress.

CATHEDRAL - The city's **Cathedral** was built towards the end of the 16th century to a design by Alessandro Pieroni, and was later enlarged in the 18th century. The simple façade is entirely faced with marble. The bell tower has a quadrangular base and is built in brick. The Latin cross interior has a single nave.

OLD FORTRESS - The **Fortezza Vecchia** is a massive brick fortification built by Antonio da Sangallo

the Younger between 1521 and 1534. Inside the fort is the small **Church of San Francesco** as well as some remains of the ancient Roman castrum.

STATUE OF THE FOUR MOORS - Situated in Piazza Giuseppe Micheli, the statue was dedicated to its central figure, Grand Duke *Ferdinando de' Medici*, made by Giovanni Bandini in 1595. However, the real sculptural masterpiece is the group of four figures – the Four Moors – four Barbary pirates in chains The four statues

GIOVANNI FATTORI CIVIC MUSEUM

The Museum dedicated to Giovanni Fattori is now located in the prestigious Villa Mimbelli, designed and built by Giuseppe Micheli between 1865 and 1875. The Museum contains, with the Gallery of Modern Art in Palazzo Pitti, the greatest number of paintings by "macchiaioli" painters. Three floors of rooms in the villa have been entirely reorganised and now exhibit, about 136 works, many of which had for long been kept in storage. In addition to the paintings of Fattori that form the main corpus of the gallery, works by Silvestro Lega, Cesare and Giovanni Bartolena, Vittorio Corcos, Michele Gordigiani, Leonetto Cappiello, Plinio Novellini and Oscar Ghiglia are displayed.

THE PROGRESSIVE MUSEUM OF CONTEMPORARY ART

Located in Villa Maria, the Museum contains works by respected contemporary artists such as Cappiello, Guttuso and Rosai.

THE YESHIVÀ MARINI JEWISH MUSEUM

The privileges established under the Livorno constitutions of 1591 and 1593 encouraged Jews to take up residence there and since then the community has always been quite numerous in the city. Exhibited in the Museum are interesting religious items and furnishings mainly from the old Synagogue of Livorno built in 1593 and destroyed during the Second World War.

were added in 1626 and are considered one of Francesco Tacca's great masterpieces.

MONTENERO SANCTUARY - In the surrounding hills is the Sanctuary of Montenero which has developed around a small chapel built in the 14th century to venerate the miraculous image of the Virgin.

SEA RESORTS NEAR LIVORNO

Castiglioncello, Rosignano, Cecina, Bibbona, Donoratico, Piombino Quercianella, Antignano, San Vincenzo

View of Livorno and its port.

THE NECROPOLI OF POPULONIA

The oldest necropoli of Populonia are located at Poggio delle Granate and San Cerbone. The tombs of the period (9th-8th cent. BC) are the classic shaft tombs (*a pozzetto*) containing only the urn with the ashes of the deceased and a few personal items. In the oriental period (7th cent. BC) there was a radical change in the types of funeral structures which tended to be more monumental, as witnessed by the chamber tombs of the **Costone della Fredda** and of the **Porcareccia**, but above all by the imposing tumuli of **St Cerbone** discovered in the early 20th century. Among the most important of the funerary monuments, mention must be made of the **Tomb of the Chariots** (dei Carri), the most imposing in the necropolis of St Cerbone. This tomb contained the remains of two war chariots with bronze and iron fittings, gold work, objects in ivory, and bronze and iron arms which date the burial to around the middle of the 7th century BC. In the **Tomb of the Cylindrical Pyxides**, the **Tomb of the Balsamario** and the **Tomb of the Pyriform Aryballos** fragments of Greek-oriental ceramics and gold and silver ornamental trinkets have been found dating them to between the middle of the 7th and beginning of the 6th century BC. Not far off is the **Tomb of the Bronzetto di Offerente** (late 6th centuary BC) an aedicule tomb, with a gabled roof. It was surrounded by a series of sarcophagi in the open air, which had already been plundered in antiquity, as is the case with most of the other tombs dating from the 5th century BC. On the Poggio della Porcareccia, between the slopes of the town and St Cerbone, are the **Tomb of the Oreficerie** (gold work), with personal ornaments in gold and silver, and the **Tomb of the Flabelli**, discovered intact, with jewellery, three magnificent fans in repoussé bronze, arms, helmets and a large quantity of bronze containers as well as Greek and local pottery. Tombs of the Hellenistic period are located at Le Grotte, Buche delle Fate and Poggio Malassarto.

SAN SILVESTRO

The **Archaeological Mining Park of San Silvestro** at Campiglia covers an area of about 450 hectares and is part of the larger system of six parks in the Val di Cornia. The most interesting aspect of this park is that all stages in the process of copper, lead and silver extraction from the origins of mining itself in the 7th century BC until the present day, may be seen here. The extensive evidence of Etruscan and Roman mining, the remains of the medieval village of San Silvestro and the tunnels opened in more recent centuries make this one of the most interesting mineral parks in all of Europe.

The Baratti Gulf near Populonia.

THE TUSCAN ARCHIPELAGO

The islands of Tuscany are scattered across the Tyrrhenian sea along the coast between Livorno and Orbetello.

They are of various sizes but, apart from the island of Elba, are generally quite small. Although increasingly popular with tourists, the flora and fauna of this group of islands has maintained an unspoilt appearance. Patches of pines, cork trees, woods of holm oaks and all those plants that constitute the Mediterranean 'macchia', including laurel, broom, myrtle, arbutus and heather, are found wherever the geological structure permits. The plants provide shelter for various species of animal such as martens, wild rabbits and goats and an environment that is a paradise for birds. The coastal depths are most popular with divers.

The islands were inhabited by Etruscans and Greeks as well as Ligurians and Carthaginians, and since ancient times have been exploited for their mineral deposits and as stopping places for pirates. The Romans built various villas on the islands and religious hermitages, often attacked by Saracen pirates, later came into being.

Island of Elba: Port of Marciana Marina (below); Portoferraio (above).

CAPRAIA (Livorno)

This small volcanic island is just eight kilometres long. It is almost completely mountainous with scanty vegetation. The island was known to the Greeks and Romans but was little frequented. It was conquered by the Saracens in 1055 and subsequently by the Pisans and then Genoans. In 1815 it was annexed to the Kingdom of Sardinia. **Capraia** is the only village on the island. The **St George Fortress**, built at the beginning of the 15th century to defend the inhabitants from invasions by Barbarian pirates, is a particularly fine structure.

ELBA (Livorno)

The largest island of the archipelago, it is about 10 kilometres from the mainland. The coast is quite beautiful with many bays and inlets all around the shoreline. The island also has many heights however, the largest being **Monte Capanne** (1019 metres).
Elba was already known to the Greeks who discovered immense

Capo d'Enfola on the island of Elba.

deposits of iron there. Later it was occupied by the Etruscans and then the Romans who left splendid villas and towns which still exist, such as **Pomonte** and **Capoliveri** *(Caput Liberum)*. In the late Middle Ages it was invaded by the Lombards and in the 11th century it came under Pisan control. In 1814 and 1815 it was independent and Napoleon was exiled here. In 1815 it was annexed to the Grand Duchy of Tuscany and in 1860 to the Kingdom of Italy.

Portoferraio - The chief town of the island, it has a small and intimate historical centre enclosed by a powerful 16th-century fortification. The centre is dominated by the **Stella Fortress**, built between 1540 and 1548 and by the **Falcone Fortress** of the same period. It is the principal port in Elba and also a noted tourist resort. Of its many fine historical buildings, mention should be made of the 16th-century **Parish church** and the **Town Hall**, which houses the **Biblioteca Comunale Foresiana**. Note also the **Church of the SS. Sacramento** and the **Church of the Misericordia** from which a small **Napoleonic Museum** is reached.

The splendid bay at Porto Azzuro.

Nearby is a monastery where the **De Laugier Centre** is located as well as the **Pinacoteca Foresiana** with a large collection of objects and many paintings dating from the 16th to the 19th centuries. Near to the town of Portoferraio are the **Villa Romana delle Grotte** (1st century BC to 1st century AD), the 12th-century Romanesque-Pisan **church of Santo Stefano delle Trane**, and the ruins of the ancient **Volterraio Castle**.

Palazzina dei Mulini - During the years of his exile on Elba from 1814-1815, Napoleon lived in the **Palazzina dei Mulini**. This quite lovely house consists of a series of rooms that include the Emperor's study, the reception hall, the footmen's room, Napoleon's dressing room, the officers' room and the library. Six kilometres from Portoferraio is the **Napoleonic villa of San Martino** where the Emperor's court lived.

Porto Azzurro - This port and village is one of the best-known seaside resorts on the island. On a small headland near to the port stands the **Portolongone** (or **St James'**) **Fortress** built in the early 17th century. The **Sanctuary of the Madonna di Monserrato**, also 17th-century, and the emerald green **Terranera lake** are near to Porto Azzurro.

The Aquarium of Marina di Campo - Elba's Aquarium is one of the most complete Mediterranean aquaria in existence. About 150 different species of Mediterranean marine life are found in the 43 tanks where their natural habitat is carefully reproduced. Many quite rare species can be seen, especially in the tropical section where genuine curiosities of marine fauna are housed. The Fauna Museum is also located inside the Aquarium, providing a reconstruction of the main natural environments on the island.

MINING ON ELBA

In addition to iron, the land of Elba is rich in many other minerals including granite, tourmaline, beryl, porphyry, quartz and marble. Mining began on the island during the Etruscan period and deposits were extracted until the 1980s when the industry ceased activity. However, it was considered necessary to preserve the memory of these thousands of years of production. In Porto Azzuro the **Piccolo Miniera** offers a trip in a small gauge train to the very heart of a mine where one can see historical items and minerals that were typical of the island. The **Museo Minerario Etrusco** provides historical information, in particular relating to the mining activity of the Etruscans on Elba.

The towns of Capoliveri, Rio Marina and Rio nell'Elba have together created the Elba Mining Park (**Parco Minerario dell'Isola d'Elba**) which offers accompanied visits to the mines in this area as well as a series of museums related to various aspects of the industry in the past: the **Museo Mineralogico elbano e dell'Arte della Miniera** at Rio Marina, the '**Alfeo Ricci' Museo dei Minerali** at Capoliveri, the **Museo Archeologico minerario** and the **Museo Minerali della Gente di Rio** in Rio nell'Elba. In a large **Amphitheatre** at Rio Marina, conferences and multimedia sessions are held on the subject and children can participate in workshops where they learn to recognise the various minerals. During the summer months a Fair and Exhibition of minerals is also held.

Marciana - The town has developed from an old village steeped in medieval, though particularly Medicean, history. Built by the Pisans, the ancient **Appiani Fortress** stands above the village. The **Archaeological Museum** is particularly interesting with much evidence of the Greek, Etruscan and Roman way of life on the island. Sights of interest near Marciana are **Borgo di Poggio**, the **Sanctuary of the Madonna del Monte** (16th century) and the **Church of San Lorenzo** in the Romanesque style of Pisa (12th century).

Aerial view of Marciana Marina.

View of Giglio Castello.

THE ISLAND OF GIGLIO
(GROSSETO)

Once occupied by the Etruscans, as documented by the remains of a ship that was wrecked in the waters of Giglio Porto, the **Villa of the Enobarbi** in the Castellari area dates, however, to Roman times. The remains of other Roman buildings have been found near Giglio Castello. The area is rich in granite, a stone much used in Roman times to build and decorate the palaces and villas of the wealthiest citizens. In 1362 the island of Giglio passed from Pisan control to Genoa and after various historic events, became a possession of Florence in 1447.

From **Giglio Porto**, a small centre clustered around its bay, the road rises steeply to the imposing **Torre del Lazzeretto** and further on to the **Faro Vecchio**. Above, the aus-tere brooding town of **Giglio Castello** appears, completely enclosed in its grey medieval walls, and with a 14th-century **Fortress** at the summit.

The Parish church is most interesting and an ivory *crucifix*, attributed to Giambologna is housed there, as well as a silver shrine containing a relic of St Maximilian, the patron saint of the island. The tiny village of **Campese** is a paradise for scuba divers.

Giannutri - The little island of Giannutri was also populated by the Romans and is still part of the commune of Giglio. There are many Roman ruins here including a majestic **Villa** dating from the 1st century AD.

The bay of Giglio Porto.

PISA

Pisa was a thriving Etruscan centre between the 6ᵗʰ and 3ʳᵈ centuries BC and at the time of Augustus it became a flourishing Roman colony (Julia Pisana Obsequens).

Under the Carolingian dynasty it became part of the marchesato of Tuscany and succeeded in becoming a free commune at the beginning of the 11ᵗʰ century. This was the beginning of an extremely prosperous period in its history which lasted almost three centuries.

The city became a powerful centre thanks to the control of the seas maintained by its relentless fleet. In this period Pisa became an ally of the Normans and aided them in their conquest of Sicily. It participated in the first crusade with its ships and founded numerous merchant colonies in the East, expanding its commercial dominion. Evidence of this felicitous period are the many religious and secular buildings which sprang up in the city. Sculptors such as Nicola Pisano, his son Giovanni Pisano, and Arnolfo di Cambio all worked in Pisa. A slow but inexorable decline began in the 13ᵗʰ and 14ᵗʰ centuries, caused by the continuous clashes on land with its neighbours Lucca and Florence and on sea with its bitter rival, Genoa. It was finally defeated by the latter at Meloria in 1284. In 1509 the Medici took possession of the city. The building of the port of Livorno deprived the city of its vital link with the sea. In 1860, Pisa became part of the Kingdom of Italy.

THE WALLS - The walls of Pisa were begun by the consul Cocco Griffi in 1155. Most probably the four gates completed in 1161 were the **Porta Legazia** and the **Calcesana**, which are quite similar and are still standing, the **Spina Alba**, now destroyed, but documented in old images, and the **Parlascio**. Other gates were later made in the walls, including the **Leone** gate, **Postierla di Santo Stefano** and **San Zeno**.

PIAZZA DEI MIRACOLI – Also known as Piazza dei Miracoli (Miracles), Pisa's cathedral square is situated in the north western corner of the city near to the **Porta del Leone** (Lion's Gate). The square developed over a long period of time, taking form between the mid 11ᵗʰ century and the mid 14ᵗʰ century. The original architectural arrangement, conceived by Buscheto, was continued by various architects: Rainaldo lengthened the cathedral; Diotisalvi established the design of the **Baptistery** and Nicola Pisano completed it; Bonanno initiated the **Bell Tower**; Giovanni di Simone saw work on it almost through to conclusion and was also responsible for planning the longer sides of the square with the **Camposanto** and the **Hospital**, which was begun in 1257.

CATHEDRAL - The cathedral of Pisa was built during the second half of the 11ᵗʰ century and was probably completed in 1118 when it was consecrated by Pope Gelasius II. The façade was probably already in place in 1136 when a Council of the Church was held here.

At the time, the cathedral of Pisa was certainly the largest and most impressive in western Christendom. The **façade** preserves evidence of the principal creators of the cathedral. In the first arch is the *sarcophagus-tomb of Buscheto*; above the central portal on the right, an *inscription* recalls Rainaldo, who began the façade; in the left pilaster, on the level of the pavement, is the *sepulchral inscription of Master Guglielmo*, the sculptor famous for the first pulpit of the Cathedral. The doors of the façade, no longer existing, and the *Porta di San Ranieri* in the right section of the transept were by Bonanno, the architect of the bell tower. The leaves of the latter are decorated with twenty *Stories of the Life of the Saviour* and *Scenes of Theophany*.

The **interior plan** consists of a nave and four aisles, similar to the largest early Christian basilicas in Rome, but with a projecting three-aisled transept. Women's galleries run along above the side aisles and an octagonal dome is set at the intersection of the nave and transept. A large apse terminates the central nave and also each arm of the transept. Pisa's foremost church is enhanced by the outstanding *pulpit* made by Giovanni Pisano in the first decade of the 14th century to replace one made by Guglielmo which was sent to Cagliari. The pulpit is carved with *Stories from the Lives of St. John the Baptist and Christ* in the panels, which are divided by figures of *Prophets* and *Saints*. It is one of the finest expressions of Italian Gothic sculpture. There is also a lovely ivory statue of the *Madonna* by Giovanni in the **Treasury.** The Cathedral also houses the *tomb of Arrigo VII* by Tino di Camaino and

the *tomb of St Ranieri*, patron saint of Pisa, is also of interest.

THE LEANING TOWER - In the mid 19th century in the course of work to reveal the sunken base of the bell tower, a broken urn with the name of Bonanno was found and is now set into the wall at the entrance. Previously known as a sculptor, the artist was thus also recognised as the architect of the bell tower. This discovery gave credit to the theory that he wished to be buried at the foot of his creation. At first the tower must simply have sunk down into the ground, but later it began to lean. Therefore in 1185, when the tower had arrived halfway up the third storey, the work was interrupted. Building began anew in 1275 under the direction of Giovanni di Simone and in only nine years another three and a half floors were raised, but work was again suspended due to difficulties. Around the middle of the 14th century Tommaso Pisano was commissioned to terminate the tower with the present belfry. Between 1990 and 2001 work was carried out to consolidate the structure and make it safe.

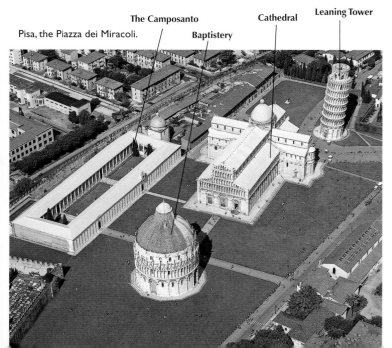

Pisa, the Piazza dei Miracoli.

The Camposanto · Baptistery · Cathedral · Leaning Tower

The cathedral with the Leaning Tower in the background.

The interior is an enormous cylindrical shaft, around which is the stairway allowing access to the external - and quite open and unprotected - loggias. A narrow stair leads to the belfry at the top of the tower. The decoration reflects that of the cathedral by Rainaldo. The entrance portal is flanked by unusual *zoomorphic engravings* and has a lunette above with a 15th century *Madonna and Child* by Andrea Guardi. Another engraving represents the *Entrance to the Port of Pisa*.

BAPTISTERY - An inscription on the pillar to the left of the entrance to Pisa's Baptistery records that it was begun in 1152 by Diotisalvi; the date is opposite. In 1260, under the direction of Nicola Pisano, the gallery of small columns was added and he also designed the Gothic facing. In 1284 Giovanni Pisano also worked on the external decoration. After the middle of the 14th century the conclusive phase in the construction of the Baptistery went into effect when it was decided to cover the building with a dome.

Although the **exterior** of the Baptistery has a two-colour scheme similar to other monuments in Pisa, the most important decorative element is the sculptural work. Examples are the decoration of the portals, especially the main portal which was given a *Madonna* by Giovanni Pisano in the lunette, and the rich decoration of the galleries where the *human heads* (now replaced by copies) at the imposts of the arches were mainly by Nicola and Giovanni Pisano.

The imposing **internal** plan of the Baptistery of Pisa is circular and the interior consists of an circular nave covered with vaulting which rests on columns and piers. Over the nave there is a women's gallery. An inscription records that the *baptismal font* of 1246 was made by Guido Bigarelli of Como. It consists of a large octagonal basin for full-immersion baptisms and four smaller fonts for baptising babies. Completing the furnishings of the Baptistery is the *pulpit* dated 1260, by Nicola Pisano; his son Giovanni and Arnolfo di Cambio seem also to have worked on it. Hexagonal in form, it stands on seven slender columns resting on lions and a high plinth. The columns support trilobate arches with figures of *Prophets* and *Evangelists*, while above the capitals are *allegorical figures* and *Saints*. *Stories of the life of Christ* are sculpted in the five sections of the parapet, divided by small columns.

THE CAMPOSANTO MONUMENTALE - The Camposanto was begun in 1278 to a design by Giovanni di Simone and consists of a rectangular gallery around the field of the old cemetery. The interior walls of the Camposanto were frescoed, especially in the 14th century, and other tombs were added to those of the illustrious Pisans. At the beginning of the 18th century antique sarcophagi, many of which had been used as tombs in the cathedral grounds, were

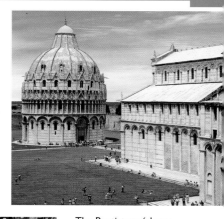

The Baptistery (above and below) and the interior of the cathedral with the marble pulpit by Giovanni Pisano.

transferred here. In the 19th century ancient and medieval material found in the city was also housed here so that today the Camposanto is one of the most important museums in Pisa. In the southern gallery the fresco paintings by Taddeo Gaddi illustrating the *Stories of Job* (14th century) are worthy of note. The 14th-century frescoes portraying the *Triumph of Death* and *Universal Judgement*, attributed to Bonamico Buffalmacco are particularly interesting. Hanging above the entrance to the west gallery are the chains that closed the entrance to the port of Pisa, removed by the Genoese in 1362. Of the numerous tombs here, that of Bartolomeo Medici, generally attributed to Il Tribolo (16th century) is worth noting. Recent reorganization has returned the frescoes of Lomi and Ghirlanda (16th-17th centuries) to their original position.

In the northern gallery 14th-century frescoes of the Umbria school portraying *Episodes from the Book of Genesis* can be seen. From the **Ammannati Chapel,** with the *funerary monument to Ligo Ammannati*, we enter the room where important detached frescoes from the southern gallery are exhibited. In the 14th-century **Aulla Chapel** is a fine painted terracotta attributed to Giovanni della Robbia (16th century). The **Sarcophagus of the Muses**, dated 3rd century is an important imperial Roman work.

101

The Camposanto in Pisa.

MUSEO DELLE SINOPIE - This museum is housed in the **Spedale Nuovo**, built between 1257 and 1286 by Giovanni di Simone. Exhibited on the first floor are the preparatory drawings of frescoed masterpieces by Bonamico Buffalmacco, such as the *Stories of the Church Fathers*, the *Universal Judgement*, the *Triumph of Death*. Proceeding, we reach a beautiful *crucifix* by the famous Pisan master, Francesco Traini, and continuing, the impressive *Annunciation* also by Buffalmacco. On the ground floor are stories from the *Old and New Testaments* by Benozzo Gozzoli.

MUSEO DELL'OPERA DEL DUOMO - This is one of the richest and most famous museums in Tuscany. Exhibited on the ground floor are numerous sculptures dating from the 11th to 12th centuries, including masterpieces by Tino di Camaino and Nino Pisano. In the centre of one particularly large and spacious room the famous **Cathedral Treasury** is on display including the magnificent *Madonna* in ivory by Giovanni Pisano, Limoges reliquaries (12th century) and numerous items of sacred items in gold. On the

first floor are many paintings dating from the 16th to 17th centuries. Also exhibited in the museum is an excellent collection of inlayed wood and illuminated manuscripts of the 12th and 13th centuries.

MUSEO NAZIONALE DI SAN MATTEO - Some of the most important exhibits here are medieval ceramics including many bowls and basins from the entire area of the Mediterranean and from Islamic countries. Pisan painting of the 12th and 13th centuries is represented by several valuable pieces such as the *Calci Bible* (12th century), a fine example of an illuminated codex; the *painted crosses* including the *St Matthew Cross* by Giunta di Capitino and the *Fucecchio Cross* by Berlinghiero.

Among the 14th-century paintings, two of the most outstanding pieces are the lovely *Polyptych* that Simone Martini made for the church of St Catherine, and the *Crucifix* by Luca di Tommè.

Some of the finest sculptures here are the works by Nicola and Giovanni Pisano, Tino di Camaino and also Andrea and Nino Pisano who were responsible for the beautiful *Madon-*

na del Latte, originally in the church of Santa Maria della Spina. There are also an excellent *Saint Paul* on a gold ground by Masaccio, *Madonna and Child* by Fra' Angelico, a *Madonna dell'Umiltà* by Gentile da Fabriano and *Madonna and Child with Saints* by Domenico Ghirlandaio. Of the 15th-century sculptural works, one of the most outstanding is the splendid *bust of San Lussorio* fused in bronze, chased and gilded, a marvellous work by Donatello originally in the church of Santo Stefano dei Cavalieri.

CHURCH OF SANTA MARIA DELLA SPINA - Previously an Oratory dedicated to Santa Maria di Pontenovo it was extended and took on its present appearance in 1323. The name is derived from the reliquary, once housed here and now in the church of Santa Chiara, of a thorn from Christ's crown. On the exterior was a *Virgin and Child*, the original of which is now in the National Museum. One of Nino Pisano's finest works was in this church and is now also housed in the National Museum, though original statues by Andrea and Nino Pisano are still on the altar.

Above, *Stories of Esau and Jacob* by Benozzo Gozzoli in the Museo delle Sinopie. Above, detail of the *Triumph of Death*, a fresco in the Camposanto by Piero di Puccio.

St Sebastian by Ghirlandaio in the San Matteo Museum.

PIAZZA DEI CAVALIERI - This square is one of the most theatrical urban creations of the Medicean period. Cosimo I had it made for the new headquarters of the Knights of Santo Stefano, an order that he had created in 1561 to defend the coasts of the Mediterranean from invasion by the Turks. The new aspect of the square was designed by Vasari after 1562, rebuilding the surrounding palaces in the new Mannerist style. The **church of Santo Stefano dei Cavalieri**, designed by Vasari between 1565 and 1569 and replacing an earlier medieval church, is situated on the square. Beside is the spectacular façade of **Palazzo dei Cavalieri** which was created by Vasari's remodelling of the Palazzo degli Anziani. Housed here is the prestigious **Scuola Normale Superiore** a university post-graduate school where famous personalities such as Carducci, Pascoli, Fermi and Rubbia studied.

THE SAINT OF SAN ROSSORE

An area that was only reclaimed from the sea in fairly recent times, the estate of San Rossore extends across the boroughs of Pisa, Vecchiano, San Guiliano Terme, Massarosa and Viareggio. The name is derived from the Christian martyr Luxorius, killed in Sardinia at the time of Diocletian's persecution. His body was brought to Pisa and it was later decided that a small church should be built in his name, though the pronunciation was later transformed into 'Rossore'.

SEA RESORTS NEAR PISA

Marina di Vecchiano
Marina di Pisa
Tirrenia
Calambrone

View of San Miniato in the province of Pisa.

SAN MINIATO

Originally in the possession of Federico Barbarossa, San Miniato, also known as San Miniato al Tedesco was an independent commune in the 14th century and then came under Florence.

The majestic **tower of Frederick** (Barbarossa) rises high above the houses while further down, but still overlooking the town, stands the **Cathedral**. Its building dates from the 13th century and at a later date **Mathilda's Tower**, once an integral part of the fortifications, was absorbed as the bell tower. The **Museo Diocesano** has been opened next to the church and it contains many works from other churches in the diocese. But the religious building which best preserves its original features is probably the **Dominican Church** dedicated to Saints James and Lucy, which dates to 1330. In the **Samminiati Chapel** is the **tomb of Giovanni Chellini**, by Bernardo Rossellino, while in the **Armaleoni** chapel is a fresco by Masolino and a panel painting by the Master of San Miniato. The **Town Hall** (Palazzo Comunale), built in the 14th century, has extensive frescoes in the **Council Chamber** by Cenni di Francesco di Ser Cenni and numerous coats of arms of the council members.

VOLTERRA

Known as Velathri, the city was for a long time one of the most powerful districts (an area ruled by a 'lucumo') of Etruria and was the last to fall to Rome after a siege lasting two years (81-80 BC). The city assumed considerable power once more between the 12th and 14th centuries when it was frequently in conflict with Pisa, Florence, Siena and San Gimignano for territorial reasons. In 1340 it became the property of the Belforti and in 1361 fell to the Florentines; thereafter its history was influenced by that of the Tuscan Grand Duchy.

Cathedral - The cathedral dates from the 12th century and has a beautiful *Pulpit* by a follower of Guglielmo Pisano. On the main altar is a an important marble *ciborium* by Mino da Fiesole who is probably also the author of the two angels on the columns on either side. In the left aisle is the **Cappella dell'Addolorata**, with the *journey of the Magi* by Benozzo Gozzoli.

THE SHADOW OF THE EVENING

Originally in the Florentine collection of the Buonarroti family and acquired by Guarnacci around 1750, this slender little bronze found near Volterra was probably a votive figure (2nd century BC). Little more than 50 centimetres in height, it became the symbol of Volterra and was named the 'Shadow of the Evening' by Gabriele D'Annunzio.

The octagonal-shaped **Baptistery** is a 13th-century Romanesque building of great architectural interest that stands in front of the cathedral.

The Pinacoteca and Civic Museum – the museum is located in the rooms of **Palazzo Minucci Solaini**, and

The Medieval centre of Volterra.

contains works by many renowned artists including an *Annunciation* (1491) and *Madonna and Child with Saints* by Luca Signorelli; a tryptych by Taddeo di Bartolo; a painting of *Saint Sebastian with Saints Bartholomew and Nicholas of Bari* by Neri di Bicci (1478); a magnificent *Deposition* by Rosso Fiorentino (1521); *Christ with Saints Benedict, Romuald, Athina and Grecina* by Ghirlandaio; a wonderful *Madonna and Child with Saints* by Volterrano.

Museo Guarnacci - The Etruscan collection in this museum is one of the most important in Italy. It was created in 1732 by cardinal Franceschini with a collection of cinerary urns and was gradually enriched with items of great archaeological value. The museum also includes a **pre-historic section** with material from the Bronze Age and tombs from the Iron Age; an **Etruscan section**, the most important both in quantity and quality, and lastly the **Roman section** with sculptures, engravings, coins, jewellery and ceramics. The most enchanting exhibit is the *Shadow of the Evening*, a slender and enigmatic little bronze figure dating from the 2nd century BC.

The Fortress and Fiumi Park - The large **Rocca-Fortezza** rises at one end of the historical centre and for many centuries was used as a prison. The structure consists of two elements that were once separate: the **Old Fort** (*Rocca Antica* or *femmina*) which dates to 1343 and which rises at one side of the Selci gate, and the **New Fort** (*Rocca Nuova* or *maschio*) which Lorenzo il Magnifico had built later (between 1472 and 1475). Near to the Fortress is the **Fiumi Park**, with interesting remains of the Etruscan acropolis with temples, roads and wells, much of which is still to be explored by further excavation.

Roman Theatre and Baths - What remains of the imposing **Roman Theatre** dating to the 1st century B.C. lies on the north side of the city. A good part of the *scenae* and of the *cavea* and the really fine portico are fairly well preserved. The **Baths**, which have mostly disappeared, were near the portico.

THE TERRACES OF VOLTERRA

In the area surrounding Volterra are quite fascinating precipices which have determined the nature of this city since the most ancient of times. The writer Giorgio Batini has described the "balze" of Volterra as representing an "astonishing phenomenon of erosion, an amazing gash in the earth, an enormous and ghastly spectacle of shocking scenery. The spectacle is centred around the "capital" of this Tuscan land where the Valdera and Val di Cecina basins meet and form the hallmark, the most flamboyant symbol of a singular territory where clay, sand and rock create unique landscapes, here consisting of continuous rolling hills and soft rises, sometimes covered by the green grass of meadows and herbaceous plants, and there of bare and arid knolls, steep valleys covered with bushes, with clefts, fissures, with gorges, gullies and ravines, and those odd little white humps or plugs that rise amidst the green crags, those white rocks that can be seen in the landscapes of the background to the 'Madonna dell'Umiltà' by Giovanni di Paolo, that Sienese painter of fairytale scenes."

The Malaspina Castle in Massa.

MASSA-CARRARA

MASSA

Situated on one of the low hills which lie below the narrow valley of the Frigido river, at the foot of the Apuan Alps, Massa is about five kilometres from the sea. The city contains various interesting examples of medieval and Renaissance architecture. The first documentary reference to the town dates from the 9th century. The first nucleus developed around the **castle of the Malaspina**, a noble family who held power in the city from 1442 to 1741. Between the 13th and the 15th centuries it was often contested by Florence, Pisa and Lucca. In 1741, with the marriage of Maria Teresa Cybo di Malaspina and Ercole III of Este, Massa became annexed to the Duchy of Este. In 1796 it became part of the estate of Elisa Baciocchi. In 1815, after the Congress of Vienna, it again came under the rule of the Este family. In 1859 it was united with the Kingdom of Sardinia and subsequently to the Kingdom of Italy.

The façade (left) and a detail of Palazzo Cybo Malaspina (below).

The obelisk in Piazza degli Aranci in the old centre of Massa.

PALAZZO CYBO MALASPINA- The Palazzo Cybo Malaspina was begun in 1557 on what remained of an earlier villa of the Malaspina family. The façade is elegantly coloured and enhanced with finely sculpted busts. It has a large internal courtyard with two storeys of loggias designed by G. F. Bergamini.

CATHEDRAL – originally 13th-century but heavily remodelled and restored in the course of time. The **façade** was remade in 1936. The **interior** is in a pleasant, light baroque style with a single large nave flanked by a series of side chapels. A 13th-century wooden *crucifix* and six magnificent bronze *candelabra* by Pietro Tacca are housed here. The **chapel of the Holy Sacrament** consists of a baroque *altar* by Alessandro Bergamini at the centre of which is a fresco of the *Madonna* by Pinturicchio and a tryptych attributed to the school of Filippo Lippi and a *crib* by Benedetto Buglioni. The atmospheric **Sepolcreto dei Cybo Malaspina** is reached form the church, an underground chamber where the sepulchral urns of the princes and dukes of Massa were housed.

CRUCIFIX BY MICHELANGELO - Housed in the church of San Rocco, an ancient religious building in Massa that has been frequently altered over the centuries, is a beautiful Crucifix considered to be an early work by Michelangelo.

ROCCA - Although the correct name is the Malaspina Castle it is now commonly known as the "Rocca". More or less triangular in shape, the central nucleus is the oldest, with a range of fine coloured marble decorations that enhance the windows and cornices. A system of fortifications with ramparts surrounds the palace which is connected by a loggia to the medieval nucleus. The long passages around the walls provide an excellent view across the town. The **Castle Museum** is open to the public and exhibits items from the Palaeolithic to the Roman periods.

THE CAVE OF WINDS

In the territory of the Apuan Alps not far from Fornovolasco in a most beautiful area still almost entirely unspoilt, known as the "Massiccio delle Piane" (Massif of the Plains) the Cave of Winds is situated. In this vast open cave it is possible to see some fascinating geological features: bare channels polished by the flow of water alongside collapsed caverns, small lakes in vertiginous chasms, framed by an incredibly stark landscape of stalactites and stalagmites. The cave is reached from Gallicano, then ascending the Turrite Secca valley as far as the little village of Fornovolasco. From here a road of about two and a half kilometres leads directly to the caves.

CARRARA

Separated from Massa by the Candia hills, Carrara lies at the foot of the Apuan Alps. This is the centre for marble and the vast quarries have been known for over two thousand years. Already in use at the fall of the Roman Empire, it became the property of the bishops of Luni. For a brief period in the 12th century Carrara succeeded in proclaiming itself a free commune but was soon absorbed by the city of Lucca, then by the Spinola of Genoa, the Scaligeri of Verona and the Visconti of Milan. In 1442, together with Massa it became part of the domain of the Malaspina and henceforth its history was united with its sister town.

PALAZZO CYBO MALASPINA - The building on Piazza Gramsci has a 16th-century layout and incorporates an earlier medieval castle of which the **keep still remains.**
Some interesting items are displayed in the courtyard, including the collection of sculptures from Luni and the famous *Fantiscritti Shrine*, a Roman altar with bas-relief sculpted figures on which the names of great artists from the past are engraved, such as Canova and Giambologna, who visited the quarry where the shrine was found.
The Palazzo is also the seat of the **Accademia delle Belle Arti** where there is a small art gallery.

CATHEDRAL - Next to the *fountain of Andrea Doria*, or the *Giant*, a lovely unfinished work by Baccio Bandinelli, is the Cathedral, begun in the 11th century and completed two centuries later. It is entirely faced with grey and white marble and is partly Romanesque and partly Gothic. The 13th-century **bell tower** is a fine example of Ligurian architecture.
The tripartite interior of the church is decorated with 12th- and 13th-century *frescoes* and important sculptures.
Beside the Cathedral is the **Baptistery-Oratory**, with a hexagonal basin and lovely baptismal font, both 16th century.

Right, a gravel river bed between the quarries and rock faces.
Above, Piazza Alberica in Carrara.

THE APUAN ALPS

Covering 54,327 hectares, the Natural Park of the Apuans is the largest protected area in Tuscany, located between the provinces of Massa Carrara and Lucca. It was created in 1985 by the Tuscan Region to protect an environment that was threatened by the excessive exploitation of the marble quarries. The Apuan Alps have been famous for centuries for their vast marble quarries and are today the major centre of production in the world. They are also very popular with walkers and climbers as there are various routes along the mountain slopes, following pathways that were created for transporting marble, while fascinating new itineraries may be followed using the network of paths and shelters created by the CAI (Italian Climbers Club).

MARBLE MUSEUM OF CARRARA

Exhibited in modern pavilions is an extensive range of marbles from the Apuan Alps, as well as a description of the various aspects of extraction, transportation and dressing of marble.

The sheer faces of the marble quarries have profoundly altered the appearance of the Apuan Alps. Left, image of the Accademia delle Belle Arti in Carrara.

110

THE GARFAGNANA AND THE "ETRUSCAN ROAD"

The Garfagnana is a lush green valley lying between two mountain ranges that are geologically very different: the Apuan Alps, bare and bleak, and the Apennines, softer and gentler with rich vegetation and woodland. The area has much of interest to see and visit, not only for its natural beauty but also because the various civilizations and populations that lived here in the past have left important evidence of their presence. The Garfagnana was inhabited as early as the Bronze Age by both local peoples and settlers from the Po Valley, as is evident from the settlement at **Fossa Nera**, near Porcari (13th-12th century BC), and was gradually taken over by the Etruscans who used the Serchio Valley for the transportation of goods inland, reaching the Lunigiana along the Aulella Valley, and reach Marzabotto

and Bologna via the Lima and Reno Valley.
Archaeological finds have been made on this route at Ponte a Moriano and, further north, close to Borgo a Mozzano, is the **Antro della Paura** (Cavern of Fear) at Gioviano; also nearby is the **Buca di Castelvenere** where sacred rituals took place, as is evident from the numerous bisexual and female bronze figurines found there.
The most important items found in this area are housed in the **Garfagnana Archaeological Museum** in Castelnuovo dei Garfagnana and in the **Civic Museum of Barga**.

Above, the peaks of the Pania di Corfino.
Below, one of the stele statues housed in the Museum in Pontremoli.

THE LUNIGIANA AND ITS HISTORY

Although in the past the Lunigiana covered a much larger area, today it consists of the mountainous zone lying between Monte Grottero and the Magra river, and the chain beginning in the same place but continuing to La Nuda and from there, across the mouth of the Carpinelli river and Monte Cavallo, reaching the Apuans. The Lunigiana, named after the ancient Roman colony of Luni, was already inhabited in prehistoric times as is clear from the number of unusual sculptures, known as "stele-statues" found in this territory and the oldest examples of which date from the Chalcolithic Age. These fascinating artefacts, rectangular in shape and engraved on the front with human features, are exhibited in the **Lunigiana Museum of Stele-Statues** in Pontremoli. Other interesting items regarding life in the area from prehistoric times are housed in the **Museo del Territorio dell'Alta Valle Aulella** at Casola in Lunigiana. During the Middle Ages, the area was divided between numerous lordships such as the Malaspina and the various surrounding states of Florence, Genoa and Milan. The entire territory is dotted with interesting medieval villages and little towns where an illustrious past is evident. The numerous impressive castles of the Malaspina still survey the entire area.

111

LUCCA

The city has ancient origins dating back to pre-Roman times; first the Ligurians and later the Etruscans settled here.

*Lucca was an important municipality in Roman times and today's Via San Gerolamo, Via Beccheria, Via Santa Lucia and Via del Moro cor-*respond to the old city cardo, *while* Via San Paolino and Via Santa Croce *were the* decumanus. *Other important remains of the Roman period are the amphitheatre and the ruins of the defensive walls, though these are severely damaged.*
The city prospered under the Lombards who created the Via Francigena, a road that brought flourishing trade and turned Lucca into the capital of Tuscia. The Carolingians followed the Lombards and the first German emperors created the Marquisate of Tuscany and chose Lucca as their principle headquarters. In 1119 the city was recognised as a free commune and its silk indus-try became renowned throughout the world. In 1314 the city was seized by the tyrant of Pisa, Ugu-cione della Faggiola, though it was subsequently governed by Castruccio Castracani who succeeded in bring-ing power and prestige to the city. On the death of Castracani Lucca experi-enced a long period of greatly disputed rule. During the 19th century Lucca once more became a rich and power-ful city under the enlightened guidance of Marie Louise Bourbon from Parma. With the plebiscite of 1860, the city be-came part of the kingdom of Italy.

The *tomb of Ilaria del Carretto*, a masterpiece by Jacopo della Quercia in the sacristy of Lucca cathedral.

View of the walls of Lucca, still perfectly intact and providing a pleasant walk along the tree-lined ramparts.

CATHEDRAL OF SAINT MARTIN – Bishop Anselmo da Baggio decreed its construction in 1060 and it was begun in the 12th century in Romanesque style, but was completely remodelled in the 14th and 15th centuries, its appearance today is therefore Gothic. The **façade** however, has remained largely Romanesque. The tripartite **interior**, with a women's gallery, has important works of art such as the statue of *St. John the Evangelist* by Jacopo della Quercia; a *Virgin and Child with Saints* by Ghirlandaio, and a magnificent *Last Supper* by Tintoretto. The sublime *Tomb of Ilaria del Carretto*, one of the finest masterpieces of Jacopo della Quercia, is now in the Sacristy. In the left nave is the famous **Tempietto** (1484) by Civitali, where a wooden crucifix dated 11th-12th centuries, mentioned by Dante in the Inferno is housed. Alongside, in the **Cathedral Museum,** is the Treasury containing numerous works of 14th and 15th century sacred gold and silverwork.

CHURCH OF SAN MICHELE IN FORO – Begun in 1143 and completed in the 14th century, this is one of the finest examples of Pisan-Luccan Romanesque architecture. The **façade** has marble decorations of the highest quality, including the outstanding figure of *Saint Michael killing the dragon*. The solid **bell tower** is also extremely fine. The church contains notable works of art such as an enamelled terracotta by Andrea della Robbia; a magnificent panel painting with *Four Saints* by Filippino Lippi; a *Virgin and Child* by Raffaello da Montelupo and lastly, on the high altar is a *Crucifix* made in Lucca in the 13th century.

CITY WALLS – Twelve metres high with 12 bastions and 11 ramparts, the walls were built between the 16th and 17th centuries to extend and renew the earlier circle of walls. Almost 5 kilometres in length, the walls are still completely intact.

Piazza dell'Anfiteatro showing the unusual form that follows the outline of the Roman amphitheatre.

GUINIGI HOUSES – This group of houses and medieval towers dates from the 14th century. The highest tower has become one of the best known symbols of Lucca. Opposite this palace is another of the same family, built around the same time, with a magnificent portico on the ground floor and with elegant two- and three-light windows over the façade.

AMPHITHEATRE SQUARE – One of the most characteristic in the city, this square is framed by a circle of old houses and is named after the Roman amphitheatre dated 2nd century AD over which it has been built. Some of the original external arches can still be seen.

Lucca cathedral and the bell tower.

TORRE DEL LAGO

The small town, situated between the Massaciuccoli lake and the Tyrrhenian sea, became famous in the early 1900s when the composer **Giacomo Puccini** (1858-1924), who was born in Lucca, built his residence on the shores of the lake. The **villa** of the composer lies only a few metres from the water and contains musical and hunting mementos of the master in the shady rooms, furnished in the Art Nouveau style then so fashionable. The statue in the small square overlooking the lake is dedicated to Puccini. Every summer in Torre del Lago the *Puccini Festival*, an interesting opera season, takes place during which the great composer's most famous operas are performed, from La *Bohème* to *Tosca*, from *Madame Butterfly* to *Turandot*. The Puccini Festival began in 1930 at the express wish of the composer who intended his operas to be enjoyed in the magnificent setting of the Massaciuccoli lake.

The statue of Puccini at Torre del Lago (above), Massaciuccoli Lake (right).

CARTOON MUSEUM (Museo del Fumetto)

The former Lorenzini military barracks is on Piazza San Romano in Lucca and houses the Italian museum of cartoon art. Lucca has for many years been the capital of cartoon art due to the international cartoon festival, Luccacomics, held here every year in October. The museum has a historic section where the original drawings of artists are displayed as well as the relevant cartoon publications; other material on display is rotated so that the entire holdings of the museum are continually renewed. There is also a virtual section where a database of cartoons can be consulted as well as the Guide to Italian Cartoons containing a catalogue and history of this art.

VILLA GUINIGI NATIONAL MUSEUM

Built in 1418, the central part of the villa has a spectacular loggia. It has been a museum since 1968 and contains an archaeological section, with artefacts from the Etruscan, Roman and Ligurian periods, as well as a prestigious artistic section with a wealth of paintings, sculptures, and minor arts that together form a compendium of art in Lucca over the centuries.
Some of the most interesting items are the sculptures of Civitali and Baccio da Montelupo, and paintings by Puccinelli, Aspertini, Pompeo Batoni and Zacchia the Elder.

The beach at Marina di Massa.

VERSILIA

A famous tourist area on the Tuscan coast since the early 1900s. Amongst the towns here are **Viareggio** which is not only an important resort, but also has an active fishing port and ship yard, and **Forte dei Marmi**, the most elegant tourist centre of the Versilia coast and one of the most famous holiday resorts in Italy.

A view of Villa Cittadella (now Grabau) and gardens.

THE VILLAS OF LUCCA

Between the 15th and 19th centuries many villas were built by wealthy families of Lucca in the hills surrounding the plain. Over three hundred are still to be found in the countryside around Lucca. Of particular artistic and historical interest are the Bernardini, Grabau, Mansi, Oliva, Reale and Torrigiani villas, which open to the public during the year.

Above and below, floats and masks at the famous carnival of Viareggio.

TRADITIONAL EVENTS

The event most closely bound to traditions and local life is without doubt the **Palio of Siena**, a horse race that takes place twice a year in the Piazza del Campo.

Just as popular, but this time in the city of Florence, is the **Scoppio del Carro** (Explosion of the Cart), a picturesque celebration which takes place during Easter

mass in the cathedral. The game of **historic football** is also Florentine. The competition is between the four historic districts of the city in the month of June and celebrates the historic football game played on 17 February 1530 as a challenge to Emperor Charles V, whose troops set siege to the city in order to restore Medici rule.

A scene of Florentine 'calcio storico' (historic football game).

Also quite impressive is the **Saracen Joust** in Arezzo, in which knights charge a dummy trying to strike it with their lance. The Joust is held on the Saturday before last in June and on the first Sunday in September.

In Pisa on 16 June the **San Ranieri illuminations** are delightful as the banks of the Arno are brilliantly lit with rows of candles; on the feast day of the city's patron saint, San Raniero (17 June), the **historic regatta** is held on the river Arno and the **Gioco del Ponte** (tug of war), a game with ancient origins, takes place between the two divisions of the town, the "Mezzogiorno" and "Tramontana" (north and south).

The Carnival of Viareggio is also quite famous, and the processions of decorated allegorical floats draw crowds of visitors. Throughout the region in springtime the **"bruscelli"** are celebrated – historic or religious events that are performed around a sapling in flower, representing the new season, followed by dancing. Other events worth experiencing are the **'Bear' Joust** at Pistoia, the **feast of the Holy Cross** in Lucca, the **Palio 'dei Micci'** in Querceta, the **Palio 'del Cerro'** at Cerreto Guidi, the **Palio 'dei Ciuchi'** in Incisa Valdarno and the **Festa del Grillo** (crickets) in Florence.

Above, flag bearers in Piazza della Signoria in Florence. Right, the Palio horse race in Siena. Below, the Joust of the Saracen in Arezzo.

PROTECTED NATURE RESERVES IN TUSCANY

The largest covering an area of 54,327 hectares is the **Apuan Nature Reserve** located between the provinces of Massa Carrara and Lucca created by the Region in 1985 to preserve an environment that the excessive exploitation of marble quarries had put at risk. A network of paths and shelters has been created for visitors by the CAI (Italian Climbers Club) and it

Below, the protected areas in Tuscany are shown in green. Above, fishermen's boats at anchor.

is possible to follow routes along mountain ridges, to discover caves and quarries, both abandoned and still in use. The **Migliarino, San Rossore and Massaciuccoli Nature Park** is the second largest in Tuscany with an area of 21,000 hectares. The landscape here is formed by beaches, dunes, pine woods, and areas of marsh along the coast from Viareggio to Livorno. The wildlife is especially interesting and includes wild boars, deer and many different species of birds. Next largest is the **Maremma Nature Park** on the **Uccellina** mountains.

It can be entered from a visitors' centre in Alberese where routes begin, leading through flourishing vegetation to arrive at the sea. The oldest Tuscan park is the **Bolgheri Wildlife Centre** (Rifugio Faunistico) which came into existence in 1962 at the initiative of Mario Incisa della Rocchetta, owner of the property. An amazing quantity of animals including roe deer, boars and water fowl can be seen here. Walks and hides exist in the park where visitors can observe the animals without disturbing them. The entrance is from the main road, known as the Aurelia. The **National Park of the Tuscan Archipelago** includes the islands of Capraia, Giannutri, Gorgona, and Montecristo. Montecristo may only be visited for reasons of research and study and with official authorization. Capraia is another protected island but is open to the public with a ferry connection to the port of Livorno. The **Wildlife Reserves of Burano and Orbetello** are at Capalbio and Albinia, located in two important lagoons where, from well concealed hides, it is possible to observe the fauna native to the Maremma, such as the porcupine, otter, and numerous kinds of birds. Bordering with Emilia Romagna are the **National Park of the Tuscan-Emilia Apennines** and the **National Park of Casentino-Montefalterona-Campiglia**. In the heart of the Siena region is the enormous **Val d'Orcia Protected Area**. There are many other protected nature parks worth a visit including the **Montioni Park** in the Province of Grosseto and the **Vallombrosa Nature Reserve**, near the old monastery.

Above, the Castelmarino Tower in the Uccellina Park.
Centre, the splendid coast near Piombino.
Below, a sunken road near to Sovana.

TRADITIONAL FOODS

ACQUACOTTA
(Maremma)

There is no single recipe, every homemaker seems to have her own variation. However, what all versions of *acquacotta,* that literally means "cooked water", have in common is that they all come from the poor soup that the cowherds, shepherds, coalmen or lumberjacks, seasonal workers who went to Maremma from Casentino – or people who worked far from home – prepared with what they could find in the woods. They boiled water from a stream or river, and poured it over slices of day-old bread, maybe even an egg and added a sprinkling of aged pecorino cheese. In those days *acquacotta* was based on chicory, spinach and wild garlic or asparagus, dried broad beans and maybe even mushrooms if the season was right. Today, this dish has become fashionable like other humble foods. It is made with a generous amount of chopped onion, celery and carrots, various vegetables (zucchini, broad beans, beet greens, mushrooms) and one egg per serving, dropped into the hot soup so that it barely sets. Place a slice of toasted bread in each bowl, pour the soup over it and, don't forget a sprinkling of grated pecorino cheese.

CROSTINI CON LA MILZA
(Tuscany)

The original recipe calls for spleen, but now chicken livers are more widely used. The chicken spleen and livers are sautéed with a little onion and a drop of wine. Then they are finely chopped together with anchovies and capers and put back on the stove for a few minutes, and diluted with a tablespoon or two of broth. The result is a tasty pâté to spread on toasted bread (some people add a splash of *vin santo*). Along with Tuscan salami and other cold cuts these *crostini* are the tastiest and most traditional antipasto served in local trattorias.

BISTECCA
ALLA FIORENTINA
(Tuscany)

This traditional Tuscan dish, the Florentine steak is the utmost in simplicity and yet it requires some skill in preparing – as well as first quality meat. The muscular loin of *Chianina* cattle – the finest Tuscan breed is the origin of the typical T-bone cut that cannot be less than 3 centimeters thick (and it can even be 8 or 10!) left at room temperature for two hours before use and then cooked over hot coals, 5 minutes on each side so that the outside is dark, while the inside is "rare." Another fine Tuscan breed is *Maremmana*, it is lean and has an excellent flavor, but since it tends to be a little tougher than *Chianina* it is recommended mainly for stewing and braising.

"RIBOLLITA"
(Tuscany)

Ribollita means "boiled again" and that is exactly what happens. It probably originated in the farm economy that did not allow people to throw away leftovers. Indeed, they went back on the hearth and were served the next day, after having put it back on the hearth. Like *acquacotta* and *panzanella*, *ribollita* is a humble dish made with lots of variations, according to the availability of greens and vegetables in season. The basic ingredients of this soup are potatoes, black

cabbage, beans (mashed and whole) and onion, along with other ingredients according to taste like beet greens, carrots and celery. After cooking very slowly, this liquid minestrone is poured into a tureen over thinly sliced day-old bread so the bread soaks up the liquid. The next day, the leftovers are reheated – reboiled – and become even more tasty.

PANZANELLA
(Florence, Siena)

Day-old bread, soaked in water, squeezed out, crumbled and dressed with sliced tomatoes, cucumbers, a little red onion, lots of basil, olive oil, vinegar and salt – is all there is to *panzanella*. And yet, it is a delicious and delightful summer dish when the vegetables are freshly picked and their flavors haven't been dulled in the refrigerator. It seems to be an old dish, perhaps from the sixteenth century even though the tomato was not among the ingredients back then – it was an unusual, colorful fruit that had just arrived from America. *Panzanella* was, and is, a humble, farm food and in some areas it is better by its other name *pan molle* that literally means "moist bread".

TRIPPA
(Florence)

As in the past, even today the "tripe," the less prized parts of beef such as the stomachs and intestines, are washed and boiled in water with herbs prior to being used to prepare some typical Florentine dishes. Favorite cuts are the croce and *cuffia* the spongy, rumen and the honeycomb stomach, respectively as well as the delicious *lampredotto* which is simply the stomach with dark meaty folds If the classic *trippa alla fiorentina* calls for cooking with carrot, celery, onion and a little tomato purée, there are a great many dishes to prepare with these cuts – without neglecting the tasty, spicy tripe sandwiches available in the city's outdoor markets.

BEANS
(Tuscany)

"*Al fiasco*" (in a flask), with oil, "*all'uccelletto*" (with tomato sauce), in country soups: Tuscans love their beans in all shapes and forms. And as with all truly simple dishes, it takes experience to cook them well: the ingredients are simply water (if possible spring water), garlic, sage, boiled without a lid on the pot, and the bean should not split and break but be cooked "*al dente*". The most popular bean is the white haricot, but each area has its own speciality and for true gourmets in search of a real speciality there are the yellow *zolfini* of the Valdarno and the delicate fine skinned *piattellini* from the hills and dells of Sorana.

PANFORTE
(Siena)

This is the king of Sienese sweets. Traveling through Tuscany it is available mainly during the Christmas season, but in and around Siena it is practically a staple – it is such a great favorite.

Like *ricciarelli*, *cavallucci*, *copate* and *pampepati* it is made according to a really old recipe The ingredients include small amounts of the Oriental spices that were already being imported during the Middle Ages, from cinnamon to cloves, from nutmeg to pepper. The mixture is based on honey (the original sweetener used in ancient times) that is slowly heated on the stove with sweet and bitter almonds – part crushed and part whole. Then flour, candied citron and other citrus fruits, the spices and confectioners' sugar are blended into the honey, the mixture is the spread over a sheet of wafer that lines a pan and baked in the oven, then the finished cake is sprinkled with confectioners' sugar.

OIL, WINE AND VIN SANTO

The simple and fresh cookery of Florence and Tuscany uses almost exclusively olive oil as a condiment and for cooking avoiding, with some rare exceptions, animal fats (butter and cream etc.). Tuscany is one of the most important producers of oil in the world and Tuscan oil, protected and controlled from the moment of planting the trees to pressing the olives, is light, flavoursome, easily digested and non-fat. The term "extravergine" means that the oil is from the first pressing and has a maximum acidic level of 1% (the lowest possible).

The wine produced is superb, starting with Chianti, a red DOC wine that is famous throughout the world, produced between Florence and Siena in the Chianti region, home to many famous labels. In addition to the supreme Brunello di Montalcino there are other excellent red wines ideal for drinking with roast and grilled meats (including the Florentine steak) such as Bolgheri-Sassicaia, Carmignano, Morellino di Scansano, Pomino and the Vino Nobile di Montepulciano. White DOC wines that go well with fish include the fine Vernaccia of San Gimignano, followed by Ansonica Costa dell'Argentario, the white from Empoli, Valdinievole, Pitigliano as well as the Pisan white San Torpè and Candia from the Apuan Hills. Other fine wines, both red and white, are labelled Capalbio, Colli di Luni, Cortona, Montedarlo, Montecucco, Monteregio di Massa Marittima, Orcia, Parrina, Sovana, Val d'Arbia, Val di Cornia and

Valdichiana. The best dessert wine is the Vin Santo, sweet or dry, made from grapes that are partially dried, left to age in special sealed kegs, and ideal to drink with the cantucci biscuits of Prato. The sophisticated Moscadello di Montalcino and the Aleatico from Elba and the Argentario are also good dessert wines. But be careful – the cost of the finest wines, especially if vintage years, just might be a bit of a surprise.

INDEX

to places and monuments by city and province

INDEX